THE LIGHT SHINES IN DARKNESS,
By Leo Tolstoy.

ACT I
SCENE 1

The scene represents the verandah of a fine country-house, in front of which a croquet-lawn and tennis-court are shown, also a flower-bed. The children are playing croquet with their governess. Mary Ivánovna Saryntsova, a handsome elegant woman of forty; her sister, Alexándra Ivánovna Kóhovtseva, a stupid, determined woman of forty-five; and her husband, Peter Semyónovich Kóhovtsef, a fat flabby man, dressed in a summer suit, with a pince-nez, are sitting on the verandah at a table with a samovár and coffee-pot. Mary Ivánovna Saryntsova, Alexándra Ivánovna Kóhovtseva, and Peter Semyónovich Kóhovtsev are drinking coffee, and the latter is smoking.

ALEXÁNDRA IVÁNOVNA. If you were not my sister, but a stranger, and Nicholas Ivánovich not your husband, but merely an acquaintance, I should think all this very original, and perhaps I might even encourage him, *J'aurais trouvé tout ça très gentil*;[1] but when I see that *your* husband is playing the fool--yes, simply playing the fool--then I can't help telling you what I think about it. And I shall tell your husband, Nicholas, too. *Je lui dirai son fait, ma chère.*[2] I am not afraid of anyone.

[1] I should have considered it all very pretty.

[2] I will tell him the plain fact, my dear.

MARY IVÁNOVNA. I don't feel the least bit hurt; don't I see it all myself? but I don't think it so very important.

ALEXÁNDRA IVÁNOVNA. No. You don't think so, but I tell you that, if you let it go on, you will be beggared. *Du train que cela va* ...[3]

[3] At the rate things are going.

PETER SEMYÓNOVICH. Come! Beggared indeed! Not with an income like theirs.

ALEXÁNDRA IVÁNOVNA. Yes, beggared! And please don't interrupt me, my dear! Anything a *man* does always seems right to you!

PETER SEMYÓNOVICH. Oh! I don't know. I was saying----

ALEXÁNDRA IVÁNOVNA. But you never do know what you are saying, because when you men begin playing the fool, *il n'y a pas de raison que ça finisse*.[4] I am only saying that if I were in your place, I should not allow it. *J'aurais mis bon ordre à toutes ces lubies.*[5] What does it all mean? A husband, the head of a family, has no occupation, abandons everything, gives everything away, *et fait le généreux à droite et à gauche*.[6] I know how it will end! *Nous en savons quelque chose.*[7]

[4] There is no reason for it to stop.

[5] I should put an end to all these fads.

[6] And plays the bountiful left and right.

[7] We know something about it.

PETER SEMYÓNOVICH [to Mary Ivánovna]. But do explain to me, Mary, what is this new movement? Of course I understand Liberalism, County Councils, the Constitution, schools, reading-rooms, and *tout ce qui s'en suit*;[8] as well as Socialism, strikes, and an eight-hour day; but what is this? Explain it to me.

[8] All the rest of it.

MARY IVÁNOVNA. But he told you about it yesterday.

PETER SEMYÓNOVICH. I confess I did not understand. The Gospels, the Sermon on the Mount--and that churches are unnecessary! But then how is one to pray, and all that?

MARY IVÁNOVNA. Yes. That is the worst of it. He would destroy everything, and give us nothing in its place.

PETER SEMYÓNOVICH. How did it begin?

MARY IVÁNOVNA. It began last year, after his sister died. He was very fond of her, and her death had a very great effect on him. He became quite morose, and was always talking about death; and then, you know, he fell ill himself with typhus. When he recovered, he was quite a changed man.

ALEXÁNDRA IVÁNOVNA. But, all the same, he came in spring to see us again in Moscow, and was very nice, and played bridge. *Il était très gentil et comme tout le monde.*[9]

[9] He was very nice, and like everybody else.

MARY IVÁNOVNA. But, all the same, he was then quite changed.

PETER SEMYÓNOVICH. In what way?

MARY IVÁNOVNA. He was completely indifferent to his family, and purely and simply had *l'idée fixe*. He read the Gospels for days on end, and did not sleep. He used to get up at night to read, made notes and extracts, and then began going to see bishops and hermits--consulting them about religion.

ALEXÁNDRA IVÁNOVNA. And did he fast, or prepare for communion?

MARY IVÁNOVNA. From the time of our marriage--that's twenty years ago--till then he had never fasted nor taken the sacrament, but at that time he did once take the sacrament in a monastery, and then immediately afterwards decided that one should neither take communion nor go to church.

ALEXÁNDRA IVÁNOVNA. That's what I say--thoroughly inconsistent!

MARY IVÁNOVNA. Yes, a month before, he would not miss a single service, and kept every fast-day; and then he suddenly decided that it was all unnecessary. What can one do with such a man?

ALEXÁNDRA IVÁNOVNA. I have spoken and will speak to him again.

PETER SEMYÓNOVICH. Yes! But the matter is of no great importance.

ALEXÁNDRA IVÁNOVNA. No? Not to you! Because you men have no religion.

PETER SEMYÓNOVICH. Do let me speak. I say that that is not the point. The point is this: if he denies the Church, what does he want the Gospels for?

MARY IVÁNOVNA. Well, so that we should live according to the Gospels and the Sermon on the Mount, and give everything away.

PETER SEMYÓNOVICH. But how is one to live if one gives everything away?

ALEXÁNDRA IVÁNOVNA. And where has he found in the Sermon on the Mount that we must shake hands with footmen? It says "Blessed are the meek," but it says nothing about shaking hands!

MARY IVÁNOVNA. Yes, of course, he gets carried away, as he always used to. At one time it was music, then shooting, then the school. But that doesn't make it any the easier for me!

PETER SEMYÓNOVICH. Why has he gone to town to-day?

MARY IVÁNOVNA. He did not tell me, but I know it is about some trees of ours that have been felled. The peasants have been cutting trees in our wood.

PETER SEMYÓNOVICH. In the pine-tree plantation?

MARY IVÁNOVNA. Yes, they will probably be sent to prison and ordered to pay for the trees. Their case was to be heard to-day, he told me of it, so I feel certain that is what he has gone about.

ALEXÁNDRA IVÁNOVNA. He will pardon them, and to-morrow they will come to take the trees in the park.

MARY IVÁNOVNA. Yes, that is what it leads to. As it is, they break our apple-trees and tread down the green cornfields, and he forgives them everything.

PETER SEMYÓNOVICH. Extraordinary!

ALEXÁNDRA IVÁNOVNA. That is just why I say that it must not be allowed to go on. Why, if it goes on like that, *tout y passera*.[10] I think it is your duty as a mother to *prendre tes mesures*.[11]

[10] Everything will be lost.

[11] To take measures.

MARY IVÁNOVNA. What can I do?

ALEXÁNDRA IVÁNOVNA. What indeed! Stop him! Explain to him that this cannot go on. You have your children! What sort of an example is it for them?

MARY IVÁNOVNA. Of course, it is hard; but I go on bearing it, and hoping it will pass, like his former infatuations.

ALEXÁNDRA IVÁNOVNA. Yes, but "*Aide toi et Dieu t'aidera!*"[12] You must make him feel that he has not only himself to think of, and that one can't live like that.

[12] God helps those who help themselves.

MARY IVÁNOVNA. The worst of all is that he no longer troubles about the children, and I have to decide everything myself. I have an unweaned baby, besides the older children: girls and boys, who have to be looked after, and need guidance. And I have to do it all single-handed. He used to be such an affectionate and attentive father, but now he seems no longer to care. Yesterday I told him that Ványa is not studying properly, and will not pass his exam., and he replied that it would be by far the best thing for him to leave school altogether.

PETER SEMYÓNOVICH. To go where?

MARY IVÁNOVNA. Nowhere! That's the most terrible thing about it; everything we do is wrong, but he does not say what would be right.

PETER SEMYÓNOVICH. That's odd.

ALEXÁNDRA IVÁNOVNA. What is there odd about it? It is just *your* usual way. Condemn everything, and do nothing yourself!

MARY IVÁNOVNA. Styópa has now finished at the University, and ought to choose a career; but his father says nothing about it. He wanted to take a post in the Civil Service, but Nicholas Ivánovich says he ought not to do so. Then he thought of entering the Horse-Guards, but Nicholas Ivánovich quite disapproved. Then the lad asked his father: "What am I to do then--not go and plough after all?" and Nicholas Ivánovich said: "Why not plough? It is much better than being in a Government Office." So what was he to do? He comes to me and asks, and I have to decide everything, and yet the authority is all in his hands.

ALEXÁNDRA IVÁNOVNA. Well, you should tell him so straight out.

MARY IVÁNOVNA. So I must! I shall have to talk to him.

ALEXÁNDRA IVÁNOVNA. And tell him straight out that you can't go on like this. That you do your duty, and he must do his; or if not--let him hand everything over to you.

MARY IVÁNOVNA. It is all so unpleasant!

ALEXÁNDRA IVÁNOVNA. I will tell him, if you like. *Je lui dirai son fait.*[13]

[13] I'll tell him the truth.

Enter a young priest, confused and agitated. He carries a book, and shakes hands all round.

PRIEST. I have come to see Nicholas Ivánovich. I have, in fact, come to return a book.

MARY IVÁNOVNA. He has gone to town, but will be back soon.

ALEXÁNDRA IVÁNOVNA. What book are you returning?

PRIEST. Oh, it's Mr. Renan's *Life of Jesus*.

PETER SEMYÓNOVICH. Dear me! What books you read!

PRIEST [much agitated, lights a cigarette] It was Nicholas Ivánovich gave it to me to read.

ALEXÁNDRA IVÁNOVNA [contemptuously] Nicholas Ivánovich gave it you! And do you agree with Nicholas Ivánovich and Mr. Renan?

PRIEST. No, of course not. If I really did agree, I should not, in fact, be what is called a servant of the Church.

ALEXÁNDRA IVÁNOVNA. But if you are, as it is called, a faithful servant of the Church, why don't you convert Nicholas Ivánovich?

PRIEST. Everyone, in fact, has his own views on these matters, and Nicholas Ivánovich really maintains much that is quite true, only he goes astray, in fact, on the main point, the Church.

ALEXÁNDRA IVÁNOVNA [contemptuously] And what are the many things that Nicholas Ivánovich maintains that are quite true? Is it true that the Sermon on the Mount bids us give our property away to strangers and let our own families go begging?

PRIEST. The Church, in fact, sanctions the family, and the Holy Fathers of the Church, in fact, blessed the family; but the highest perfection really demands the renunciation of worldly advantages.

ALEXÁNDRA IVÁNOVNA. Of course the Anchorites acted so, but ordinary mortals, I should imagine, should act in an ordinary way, as befits all good Christians.

PRIEST. No one can tell unto what he may be called.

ALEXÁNDRA IVÁNOVNA. And, of course, you are married?

PRIEST. Oh yes.

ALEXÁNDRA IVÁNOVNA. And have you any children?

PRIEST. Two.

ALEXÁNDRA IVÁNOVNA. Then why don't you renounce worldly advantages, and not go about smoking a cigarette?

PRIEST. Because of my weakness, in fact, my unworthiness.

ALEXÁNDRA IVÁNOVNA. Ah! I see that instead of bringing Nicholas Ivánovich to reason, you support him. That, I tell you straight out, is wrong!

Enter Nurse.

NURSE. Don't you hear baby crying? Please come to nurse him.

MARY IVÁNOVNA. I'm coming, coming! [Rises and exit].

ALEXÁNDRA IVÁNOVNA. I'm dreadfully sorry for my sister. I see how she suffers. Seven children, one of them unweaned, and then all these fads to put up with. It seems to me quite plain that he has something wrong here [touching her forehead. To Priest] Now tell me, I ask you, what new religion is this you have discovered?

PRIEST. I don't understand, in fact ...

ALEXÁNDRA IVÁNOVNA. Oh, please don't beat about the bush. You know very well what I am asking you about.

PRIEST. But allow me ...

ALEXÁNDRA IVÁNOVNA. I ask you, what creed is it that bids us shake hands with every peasant and let them cut down the trees, and give them money for vódka, and abandon our own families?

PRIEST. I don't know that ...

ALEXÁNDRA IVÁNOVNA. He says it is Christianity. You are a priest of the Orthodox Greek Church, and therefore you must know and must say whether Christianity bids us encourage robbery.

PRIEST. But I ...

ALEXÁNDRA IVÁNOVNA. Or else, why are you a priest, and why do you wear long hair and a cassock?

PRIEST. But we are not asked ...

ALEXÁNDRA IVÁNOVNA. Not asked, indeed! Why, I am asking you! He told me yesterday that the Gospels say, "Give to him that asketh of thee." But then in what sense is that meant?

PRIEST. In its plain sense, I suppose.

ALEXÁNDRA IVÁNOVNA. And I think not in the plain sense; we have always been taught that everybody's position is appointed by God.

PRIEST. Of course, but yet ...

ALEXÁNDRA IVÁNOVNA. Oh, yes. It's just as I was told; you take his side, and that is wrong! I say so straight out. If some young school teacher, or some young lad, lickspittles to him, it's bad enough--but you, in your position, should remember the responsibility that rests on you.

PRIEST. I try to ...

ALEXÁNDRA IVÁNOVNA. What sort of religion is it, when he does not go to church, and does not believe in the sacraments? And instead of bringing him to his senses, you read Renan with him, and interpret the Gospels in a way of your own.

PRIEST [excitedly] I cannot answer. I am, in fact, upset, and will hold my tongue.

ALEXÁNDRA IVÁNOVNA. Oh! If only I were your Bishop; I'd teach you to read Renan and smoke cigarettes.

PETER SEMYÓNOVICH. *Mais cessez, au nom du ciel. De quel droit?*[14]

[14] But do stop, for heaven's sake. What right have you?

ALEXÁNDRA IVÁNOVNA. Please don't teach me. I am sure the Reverend Father is not angry with me. What if I have spoken plainly. It would have been worse had I bottled up my anger. Isn't that so?

PRIEST. Forgive me if I have not expressed myself as I should. [Uncomfortable pause].

Enter Lyúba and Lisa. Lyúba, Mary Ivánovna's daughter, is a handsome energetic girl of twenty. Lisa, Alexándra Ivánovna's daughter, is a little older. Both have kerchiefs on their heads, and are carrying baskets, to go gathering mushrooms. They greet Alexándra Ivánovna, Peter Semyónovich, and the priest.

LYÚBA. Where is Mamma?

ALEXÁNDRA IVÁNOVNA. Just gone to the baby.

PETER SEMYÓNOVICH. Now mind you bring back plenty of mushrooms. A little village girl brought some lovely white ones this morning. I'd go with you myself, but it's too hot.

LISA. Do come, Papa!

ALEXÁNDRA IVÁNOVNA. Yes, go, for you are getting too fat.

PETER SEMYÓNOVICH. Well, perhaps I will, but I must first fetch some cigarettes. [Exit].

ALEXÁNDRA IVÁNOVNA. Where are all the young ones?

LYÚBA. Styópa is cycling to the station, the tutor has gone to town with papa. The little ones are playing croquet, and Ványa is out there in the porch, playing with the dogs.

ALEXÁNDRA IVÁNOVNA. Well, has Styópa decided on anything?

LYÚBA. Yes. He has gone himself to hand in his application to enter the Horse-Guards. He was horribly rude to papa yesterday.

ALEXÁNDRA IVÁNOVNA. Of course, it's hard on him too.... *Il n'y a pas de patience qui tienne.*[15] The young man must begin to live, and he is told to go and plough!

[15] There are limits to human endurance.

LYÚBA. That's not what papa told him; he said ...

ALEXÁNDRA IVÁNOVNA. Never mind. Still Styópa must begin life, and whatever he proposes, it's all objected to. But here he is himself.

The Priest steps aside, opens a book, and begins to read. Enter Styópa cycling towards the verandah.

ALEXÁNDRA IVÁNOVNA. *Quand on parle du soleil on en voit les rayons.*[16] We were just talking about you. Lyúba says you were rude to your father.

[16] Speak of the sun and you see its rays.

STYÓPA. Not at all. There was nothing particular. He gave me his opinion, and I gave him mine. It is not my fault that our views differ. Lyúba, you know, understands nothing, but must have her say about everything.

ALEXÁNDRA IVÁNOVNA. Well, and what have you decided on?

STYÓPA. I don't know what Papa has decided. I'm afraid he does not quite know himself; but as for me, I have decided to volunteer for the Horse-Guards. In our house some special objection is made to every step that is taken; but this is all quite simple. I have finished my studies, and must serve my time. To enter a line regiment and serve with tipsy low-class officers would be unpleasant, and so I'm entering the Horse-Guards, where I have friends.

ALEXÁNDRA IVÁNOVNA. Yes; but why won't your father agree to it?

STYÓPA. Papa! What is the good of talking about him? He is now possessed by his *idée fixe*.[17] He sees nothing but what he wants to see. He says military service is the basest kind of employment, and that therefore one should not serve, and so he won't give me any money.

[17] Fixed idea.

LISA. No! Styópa. He did not say that! You know I was present. He says that if you cannot avoid serving, you should go when you are called; but that to volunteer, is to choose that kind of service of your own free will.

STYÓPA. But it's I, not he, who is going to serve. He himself was in the army!

LISA. Yes, but he does not exactly say that he will not give you the money; but that he cannot take part in an affair that is contrary to his convictions.

STYÓPA. Convictions have nothing to do with it. One must serve--and that's all!

LISA. I only say what I heard.

STYÓPA. I know you always agree with Papa. Do you know, Aunt, that Lisa takes Papa's side entirely in everything?

LISA. What is true ...

ALEXÁNDRA IVÁNOVNA. Don't I know that Lisa always takes up with any kind of nonsense. She scents nonsense. *Elle flaire cela de loin.*[18]

[18] She scents it from afar.

Enter Ványa running in with a telegram in his hand, followed by the dogs. He wears a red shirt.

VÁNYA [to Lyúba]. Guess who is coming?

LYÚBA. What's the use of guessing? Give it here [stretching towards him. Ványa does not let her have the telegram].

VÁNYA. I'll not give it you, and I won't say who it is from. It's someone who makes you blush!

LYÚBA. Nonsense! Who is the telegram from?

VÁNYA. There, you're blushing! Aunty, she is blushing, isn't she?

LYÚBA. What nonsense! Who is it from? Aunty, who is it from?

ALEXÁNDRA IVÁNOVNA. The Cheremshánovs.

LYÚBA. Ah!

VÁNYA. There you are! Why are you blushing?

LYÚBA. Let me see the telegram, Aunt. [Reads] "Arriving all three by the mail train. Cheremshánovs." That means the Princess, Borís, and Tónya. Well, I am glad!

VÁNYA. There you are, you're glad! Styópa, look how she is blushing.

STYÓPA. That's enough--teasing over and over again.

VÁNYA. Of course, because you're sweet on Tónya! You'd better cast lots; for two men must not marry one another's sisters.[19]

[19] In Russia the relationships that are set up by marriage debar a marriage between a woman's brother-in-law and her sister.

STYÓPA. Don't humbug! Shut up! How often have you been told to?

LISA. If they are coming by the mail train, they will be here directly.

LYÚBA. That's true, so we can't go for mushrooms.

Enter Peter Semyónovich with his cigarettes.

LYÚBA. Uncle Peter, we are not going!

PETER SEMYÓNOVICH. Why not?

LYÚBA. The Cheremshánovs are coming directly. Better let's play tennis till they come. Styópa, will you play?

STYÓPA. I may as well.

LYÚBA. Ványa and I against you and Lisa. Agreed? Then I'll get the balls and call the boys. [Exit].

PETER SEMYÓNOVICH. So I'm to stay here after all!

PRIEST [preparing to go]. My respects to you.

ALEXÁNDRA IVÁNOVNA. No, wait a bit, Father. I want to have a talk with you. Besides, Nicholas Ivánovich will be here directly.

PRIEST [sits down, and lights another cigarette]. He may be a long time.

ALEXÁNDRA IVÁNOVNA. There, someone is coming. I expect it's he.

PETER SEMYÓNOVICH. Which Cheremshánova is it? Can it be Golitzin's daughter?

ALEXÁNDRA IVÁNOVNA. Yes, of course. It's the Cheremshánova who lived in Rome with her aunt.

PETER SEMYÓNOVICH. Dear me, I shall be glad to see her. I have not met her since those days in Rome when she used to sing duets with me. She sang beautifully. She has two children, has she not?

ALEXÁNDRA IVÁNOVNA. Yes, they are coming too.

PETER SEMYÓNOVICH. I did not know that they were so intimate with the Sarýntsovs.

ALEXÁNDRA IVÁNOVNA. Not intimate, but they lodged together abroad last year, and I believe that *la princesse a des vues sur Lyúba pour son fils. C'est une fine mouche, elle flaire une jolie dot.*[20]

[20] The princess has her eye on Lyúba for her son. She is a knowing one, and scents a nice dowry.

PETER SEMYÓNOVICH. But the Cheremshánovs themselves were rich.

ALEXÁNDRA IVÁNOVNA. They *were*. The prince is still living, but he has squandered everything, drinks, and has quite gone to the dogs. She petitioned the Emperor, left her husband, and so managed to save a few scraps. But she has given her children a splendid education. *Il faut lui rendre cette justice.*[21] The daughter is an admirable musician; and the son has finished the University, and is charming. Only I don't think Mary is quite pleased. Visitors are inconvenient just now. Ah! here comes Nicholas.

[21] One must do her that much justice.

Enter Nicholas Ivánovich.

NICHOLAS IVÁNOVICH. How d'you do, Alína;[22] and you, Peter Semyónovich. [To the Priest] Ah! Vasíly Nikanórych. [Shakes hands with them].

[22] Alína is an abbreviation, and a pet name, for Alexándra.

ALEXÁNDRA IVÁNOVNA. There is still some coffee left. Shall I give you a cup? It's rather cold, but can easily be warmed up. [Rings].

NICHOLAS IVÁNOVICH. No, thank you. I have had something. Where is Mary?

ALEXÁNDRA IVÁNOVNA. Feeding Baby.

NICHOLAS IVÁNOVICH. Is she quite well?

ALEXÁNDRA IVÁNOVNA. Pretty well. Have you done your business?

NICHOLAS IVÁNOVICH. I have. Yes. If there *is* any tea or coffee left, I will have some. [To Priest] Ah! you've brought the book back. Have you read it? I've been thinking about you all the way home.

Enter man-servant, who bows. Nicholas Ivánovich shakes hands with him. Alexándra Ivánovna shrugs her shoulders, exchanging glances with her husband.

ALEXÁNDRA IVÁNOVNA. Re-heat the samovár, please.

NICHOLAS IVÁNOVICH. That's not necessary, Alína. I don't really want any, and I'll drink it as it is.

Missy, on seeing her father, leaves her croquet, runs to him, and hangs round his neck.

MISSY. Papa! Come with me.

NICHOLAS IVÁNOVICH [caressing her]. Yes, I'll come directly. Just let me eat something first. Go and play, and I'll soon come.

Exit Missy.

Nicholas Ivánovich sits down to the table, and eats and drinks eagerly.

ALEXÁNDRA IVÁNOVNA. Well, were they sentenced?

NICHOLAS IVÁNOVICH. Yes! They were. They themselves pleaded guilty. [To Priest] I thought you would not find Renan very convincing ...

ALEXÁNDRA IVÁNOVNA. And you did not approve of the verdict?

NICHOLAS IVÁNOVICH [vexed]. Of course I don't approve of it. [To Priest] The main question for you is not Christ's divinity, or the history of Christianity, but the Church ...

ALEXÁNDRA IVÁNOVNA. Then how was it? *They* confessed their guilt, *et vous leur avez donné un démenti*?[23] They did not steal them--but only took the wood?

[23] And you contradicted them.

NICHOLAS IVÁNOVICH [who had begun talking to the priest, turns resolutely to Alexándra Ivánovna]. Alína, my dear, do not pursue me with pinpricks and insinuations.

ALEXÁNDRA IVÁNOVNA. But not at all ...

NICHOLAS IVÁNOVICH. And if you really want to know why I can't prosecute the peasants about the wood they needed and cut down ...

ALEXÁNDRA IVÁNOVNA. I should think they also need this samovár.

NICHOLAS IVÁNOVICH. Well, if you want me to tell you why I can't agree with those people being shut up in prison, and being totally ruined, because they cut down ten trees in a forest which is considered to be mine ...

ALEXÁNDRA IVÁNOVNA. Considered so by everybody.

PETER SEMYÓNOVICH. Oh dear! Disputing again.

NICHOLAS IVÁNOVICH. Even if I considered that forest mine, which I cannot do, we have 3000 acres of forest, with about 150 trees to the acre. In all, about 450,000 trees--is that correct? Well, they have cut down ten trees--that is, one 45-thousandth part. Now is it worth while, and can one really decide, to tear a man away from his family and put him in prison for that?

STYÓPA. Ah! but if you don't hold on to this one 45-thousandth, all the other 44,990 trees will very soon be cut down also.

NICHOLAS IVÁNOVICH. But I only said *that* in answer to your aunt. In reality I have no right to this forest. Land belongs to everyone; or rather, it can't belong to anyone. We have never put any labour into this land.

STYÓPA. No, but you saved money and preserved this forest.

NICHOLAS IVÁNOVICH. How did I get my savings? What enabled me to save up? And I didn't preserve the forest myself! However, this is a matter which can't be proved to anyone who does not himself feel ashamed when he strikes at another man--

STYÓPA. But no one is striking anybody!

NICHOLAS IVÁNOVICH. Just as when a man feels no shame at taking toll from others' labour without doing any work himself, you cannot prove to him that he ought to be ashamed; and the object of all the Political Economy you learnt at the University is merely to justify the false position in which we live.

STYÓPA. On the contrary; science destroys all prejudices.

NICHOLAS IVÁNOVICH. However, all this is of no importance to me. What is important is that in Yefím's[24] place I should have acted as he did, and I should have been desperate had I been imprisoned. And as I wish to do to others as I wish them to do to me--I cannot condemn him, but do what I can to save him.

[24] Yefím was the peasant who had cut down the tree.

PETER SEMYÓNOVICH. But, if one goes on that line, one cannot possess anything.

Alexándra Ivánovna and Styópa--

Both speak together

{ ALEXÁNDRA IVÁNOVNA. Then it is much more profitable to steal than to { work. { { STYÓPA. You never reply to one's arguments. I say that a man who { saves, has a right to enjoy his savings.

NICHOLAS IVÁNOVICH [smiling] I don't know which I am to reply to. [To Peter Semyónovich] It's true. One should not possess anything.

ALEXÁNDRA IVÁNOVNA. But if one should not possess anything, one can't have any clothes, nor even a crust of bread, but must give away everything, so that it's impossible to live.

NICHOLAS IVÁNOVICH. And it should be impossible to live as we do!

STYÓPA. In other words, we must die! Therefore, that teaching is unfit for life....

NICHOLAS IVÁNOVICH. No. It is given just that men may live. Yes. One should give everything away. Not only the forest we do not use and hardly ever see, but even our clothes and our bread.

ALEXÁNDRA IVÁNOVNA. What! And the children's too?

NICHOLAS IVÁNOVICH. Yes, the children's too. And not only our bread, but ourselves. Therein lies the whole teaching of Christ. One must strive with one's whole strength to give oneself away.

STYÓPA. That means to die.

NICHOLAS IVÁNOVICH. Yes, even if you gave your life for your friends, that would be splendid both for you and for others. But the fact is that man is not solely a spirit, but a spirit within a body; and the flesh draws him to live for itself, while the spirit of light draws him to live for God and for others: and the life in each of us is not solely animal, but is equipoised between the two. But the more it is a life for God, the better; and the animal will not fail to take care of itself.

STYÓPA. Why choose a middle course: an equipoise between the two? If it is right to do so--why not give away everything and die?

NICHOLAS IVÁNOVICH. That would be splendid. Try to do it, and it will be well both for you and for others.

ALEXÁNDRA IVÁNOVNA. No, that is not clear, not simple. *C'est tiré par les cheveux.*[25]

[25] It's too fine spun.

NICHOLAS IVÁNOVICH. Well, I can't help it, and it can't be explained by argument. However, that is enough.

STYÓPA. Yes, quite enough, and I also don't understand it. [Exit].

NICHOLAS IVÁNOVICH [turns to Priest] Well, what impression did the book make on you?

PRIEST [agitated] How shall I put it? Well, the historic part is insufficiently worked out, and it is not fully convincing, or let us say, quite reliable; because the materials are, as a matter of fact, insufficient. Neither the Divinity of Christ, nor His lack of Divinity, can be proved historically; there is but one irrefragable proof....

During this conversation first the ladies and then Peter Semyónovich go out.

NICHOLAS IVÁNOVICH. You mean the Church?

PRIEST. Well, of course, the Church, and the evidence, let's say, of reliable men--the Saints for instance.

NICHOLAS IVÁNOVICH. Of course, it would be excellent if there existed a set of infallible people to confide in. It would be very desirable; but its desirability does not prove that they exist!

PRIEST. And I believe that just *that is* the proof. The Lord could not in fact have exposed His law to the possibility of mutilation or misinterpretation, but must in fact have left a guardian of His truth to prevent that truth being mutilated.

NICHOLAS IVÁNOVICH. Very well; but we first tried to prove the truth itself, and now we are trying to prove the reliability of the guardian of the truth.

PRIEST. Well here, as a matter of fact, we require faith.

NICHOLAS IVÁNOVICH. Faith--yes, we need faith. We can't do without faith. Not, however, faith in what other people tell us, but faith in what we arrive at ourselves, by our own thought, our own reason ... faith in God, and in true and everlasting life.

PRIEST. Reason may deceive. Each of us has a different mind.

NICHOLAS IVÁNOVICH [hotly] There, that is the most terrible blasphemy! God has given us just one sacred tool for finding the truth--the only thing that can unite us all, and we do not trust it!

PRIEST. How can we trust in it, when there are contradictions?

NICHOLAS IVÁNOVICH. Where are the contradictions? That twice two are four; and that one should not do to others what one would not like oneself; and that everything has a cause? Truths of that kind we all acknowledge because they accord with all our reason. But that God appeared on Mount Sinai to Moses, or that Buddha flew up on a sunbeam, or that Mahomet went up into the sky, and that Christ flew there also--on matters of that kind we are all at variance.

PRIEST. No, we are not at variance, those of us who abide in the truth are all united in one faith in God, Christ.

NICHOLAS IVÁNOVICH. No, even there, you are not united, but have all gone asunder; so why should I believe you rather than I would believe a Buddhist Lama? Only because I happened to be born in your faith?

[The tennis players dispute] "Out!" "Not out!"

VÁNYA. I saw it ...:

During the conversation, men-servants set the table again for tea and coffee.

NICHOLAS IVÁNOVICH. You say the Church unites. But, on the contrary, the worst dissensions have always been caused by the Church. "How often would I have gathered you as a hen gathers her chickens." ...

PRIEST. That was until Christ. But Christ did gather them all together.

NICHOLAS IVÁNOVICH. Yes, Christ united; but we have divided: because we have understood him the wrong way round. He destroyed all Churches.

PRIEST. Did he not say: "Go, tell the Church."

NICHOLAS IVÁNOVICH. It is not a question of words! Besides those words don't refer to what we call "Church." It is the spirit of the teaching that matters. Christ's teaching is universal, and includes all religions, and does not admit of anything exclusive; neither of the Resurrection nor the Divinity of Christ, nor the Sacraments--nor of anything that divides.

PRIEST. That, as a matter of fact, if I may say so, is your own interpretation of Christ's teaching. But Christ's teaching is all founded on His Divinity and Resurrection.

NICHOLAS IVÁNOVICH. That's what is so dreadful about the Churches. They divide by declaring that they possess the full indubitable and infallible truth. They say: "It has pleased us and the Holy Ghost." That began at the time of the first Council of the Apostles. They then began to maintain that they had the full and *exclusive* truth. You see, if I say there is a God: the first cause of the Universe, everyone can agree with me; and *such* an acknowledgment of God will unite us; but if I say there is a God: Brahma, or Jehovah, or a Trinity, such a God divides us. Men wish to unite, and to that end devise all means of union, but neglect the one indubitable means of union--the search for truth! It is as if people in an enormous building, where the light from above shone down into the centre, tried to unite in groups around lamps in different corners, instead of going towards the central light, where they would naturally all be united.

PRIEST. And how are the people to be guided--without any really definite truth?

NICHOLAS IVÁNOVICH. That's what is terrible! Each *one* of us has to save *his own* soul, and has to do God's work *himself*, but instead of that we busy ourselves saving *other people* and teaching *them*. And what do we teach them? We teach them now, at the end of the nineteenth century, that God created the world in six days, then caused a flood, and put all the animals in an ark, and all the rest of the horrors and nonsense of the Old Testament. And then that Christ ordered everyone to be baptized with water; and we make them believe in all the absurdity and meanness of an Atonement essential to salvation; and then that he rose up into the heavens which do not really exist, and there sat down at the right hand of the Father. We have got used to all this, but really it is dreadful! A child, fresh and ready to receive all that is good and true, asks us what the world is, and what its laws are; and we, instead of revealing to him the teaching of love and truth that has been given to us, carefully ram into his head all sorts of horrible absurdities and meannesses, ascribing them all to God. Is that not terrible? It is as great a crime as man can commit. And we--you and your Church--do this! Forgive me!

PRIEST. Yes, if one looks at Christ's teaching from a rationalistic point of view, it is so.

NICHOLAS IVÁNOVICH. Whichever way one looks, it is so. [Pause].

Enter Alexándra Ivánovna. Priest bows to take his leave.

ALEXÁNDRA IVÁNOVNA. Good-bye, Father. He will lead you astray. Don't you listen to him.

PRIEST. No. Search the Scriptures! The matter is too important, as a matter of fact, to be--let's say--neglected. [Exit].

ALEXÁNDRA IVÁNOVNA. Really, Nicholas, you have no pity on him! Though he is a priest, he is still only a boy, and can have no firm convictions or settled views....

NICHOLAS IVÁNOVICH. Give him time to settle down and petrify in falsehood? No! Why should I? Besides, he is a good, sincere man.

ALEXÁNDRA IVÁNOVNA. But what will become of him if he believes you?

NICHOLAS IVÁNOVICH. He need not believe *me*. But if he saw the truth, it would be well for him and for everybody.

ALEXÁNDRA IVÁNOVNA. If it were really so good, everyone would be ready to believe you. As it is, no one believes you, and your wife least of all. She *can't* believe you.

NICHOLAS IVÁNOVICH. Who told you that?

ALEXÁNDRA IVÁNOVNA. Well, just you try and explain it to her! She will never understand, nor shall I, nor anyone else in the world, that one must care for other people and abandon one's own children. Go and try to explain that to Mary!

NICHOLAS IVÁNOVICH. Yes, and Mary will certainly understand. Forgive me, Alexándra, but if it were not for other people's influence, to which she is very susceptible, she would understand me and go with me.

ALEXÁNDRA IVÁNOVNA. To beggar your children for the sake of drunken Yefím and his sort? Never! But if I have made you angry, please forgive me. I can't help speaking out.

NICHOLAS IVÁNOVICH. I am not angry. On the contrary, I am even glad you have spoken out and given me the opportunity--challenged me--to explain to Mary my whole outlook on life. On my way home to-day I was thinking of doing so, and I will speak to her at once; and you will see that she will agree, because she is wise and good.

ALEXÁNDRA IVÁNOVNA. Well, as to that, allow me to have my doubts.

NICHOLAS IVÁNOVICH. But I have no doubts. For you know, this is not any invention of my own; it is only what we all of us know, and what Christ revealed to us.

ALEXÁNDRA IVÁNOVNA. Yes, you think Christ revealed this, but I think he revealed something else.

NICHOLAS IVÁNOVICH. It cannot be anything else.

Shouts from the tennis ground.

LYÚBA. Out!

VÁNYA. No, we saw it.

LISA. I know. It fell just here!

LYÚBA. Out! Out! Out!

VÁNYA. It's not true.

LYÚBA. For one thing, it's rude to say "It's not true."

VÁNYA. And it's rude to say what is not true!

NICHOLAS IVÁNOVICH. Just wait a bit, and don't argue, but listen. Isn't it true that at any moment we may die, and either cease to exist, or go to God who expects us to live according to His will?

ALEXÁNDRA IVÁNOVNA. Well?

NICHOLAS IVÁNOVICH. Well, what can I do in this life other than what the supreme judge in my soul, my conscience--God--requires of me? And my conscience--God--requires that I should regard everybody as equal, love everybody, serve everybody.

ALEXÁNDRA IVÁNOVNA. Your own children too?

NICHOLAS IVÁNOVICH. Naturally, my own too, but obeying all that my conscience demands. Above all, that I should understand that my life does not belong to me--nor yours to you--but to God, who sent us into the world and who requires that we should do His will. And His will is ...

ALEXÁNDRA IVÁNOVNA. And you think that you will persuade Mary of this?

NICHOLAS IVÁNOVICH. Certainly.

ALEXÁNDRA IVÁNOVNA. And that she will give up educating the children properly, and will abandon them? Never!

NICHOLAS IVÁNOVICH. Not only will she understand, but you too will understand that it is the only thing to do.

ALEXÁNDRA IVÁNOVNA. Never!

Enter Mary Ivánovna.

NICHOLAS IVÁNOVICH. Well, Mary! I didn't wake you this morning, did I?

MARY IVÁNOVNA. No, I was not asleep. And have you had a successful day?

NICHOLAS IVÁNOVICH. Yes, very.

MARY IVÁNOVNA. Why, your coffee is quite cold! Why do you drink it like that? By the way, we must prepare for our visitors. You know the Cheremshánovs are coming?

NICHOLAS IVÁNOVICH. Well, if you're glad to have them, I shall be very pleased.

MARY IVÁNOVNA. I like her and her children, but they have chosen a rather inconvenient time for their visit.

ALEXÁNDRA IVÁNOVNA [rising] Well, talk matters over with him, and I'll go and watch the tennis.

A pause, then Mary Ivánovna and Nicholas Ivánovich begin both talking at once.

MARY IVÁNOVNA. It's inconvenient, because we must have a talk.

NICHOLAS IVÁNOVICH. I was just saying to Aline ...

MARY IVÁNOVNA. What?

NICHOLAS IVÁNOVICH. No, you speak first.

MARY IVÁNOVNA. Well, I wanted to have a talk with you about Styópa. After all, something *must* be decided. He, poor fellow, feels depressed, and does not know what awaits him. He came to me, but how can I decide?

NICHOLAS IVÁNOVICH. Why decide? He can decide for himself.

MARY IVÁNOVNA. But, you know, he wants to enter the Horse-Guards as a volunteer, and in order to do that he must get you to countersign his papers, and he must also be in a position to keep himself; and you don't give him anything. [Gets excited].

NICHOLAS IVÁNOVICH. Mary, for heaven's sake don't get excited, but listen to me. I don't give or withhold anything. To enter military service of one's own free will, I consider either a stupid, insensate action, suitable for a savage if the man does not understand the evil of his action, or despicable if he does it from an interested motive....

MARY IVÁNOVNA. But nowadays everything seems savage and stupid to you. After all, he must live; you lived!

NICHOLAS IVÁNOVICH [getting irritable] I lived when I did not understand; and when nobody gave me good advice. However, it does not depend on me but on him.

MARY IVÁNOVNA. How not on you? It's you who don't give him an allowance.

NICHOLAS IVÁNOVICH. I can't give what is not mine!

MARY IVÁNOVNA. Not yours? What do you mean?

NICHOLAS IVÁNOVICH. The labour of others does not belong to me. To give him money, I must first take it from others. I have no right to do that, and I cannot do it! As long as I manage the estate I must manage it as my conscience dictates; and I cannot give the fruits of the toil of the overworked peasants to be spent on the debaucheries of Life-Guardsmen. Take over my property, and then I shall not be responsible!

MARY IVÁNOVNA. You know very well that I don't want to take it, and moreover I can't. I have to bring up the children, besides nursing them and bearing them. It is cruel!

NICHOLAS IVÁNOVICH. Mary, dear one! That is not the main thing. When you began to speak I too began and wanted to talk to you quite frankly. We must not go on like this. We are living together, but don't understand one another. Sometimes we even seem to misunderstand one another on purpose.

MARY IVÁNOVNA. I want to understand, but I don't. No, I don't understand you. I do not know what has come to you.

NICHOLAS IVÁNOVICH. Well then, try and understand! This may not be a convenient time, but heaven knows when we shall find a convenient time. Understand not me--but yourself: the meaning of your own life! We can't go on living like this without knowing what we are living for.

MARY IVÁNOVNA. We have lived so, and lived very happily. [Noticing a look of vexation on his face] All right, all right, I am listening.

NICHOLAS IVÁNOVICH. Yes, I too lived so--that is to say, without thinking why I lived; but a time came when I was terror-struck. Well, here we are, living on other people's labour--making others work for us--bringing children into the world and bringing them up to do the same. Old age will come, and death, and I shall ask myself: "Why have I lived?" In order to breed more parasites like myself? And, above all, we do not even enjoy this life. It is only endurable, you know, while, like Ványa, you overflow with life's energy.

MARY IVÁNOVNA. But everybody lives like that.

NICHOLAS IVÁNOVICH. And they are all unhappy.

MARY IVÁNOVNA. Not at all.

NICHOLAS IVÁNOVICH. Anyhow, I saw that I was terribly unhappy, and that I made you and the children unhappy, and I asked myself: "Is it possible that God created us for this end?" And as soon as I thought of it, I felt at once that he had not. I asked myself: "What, then, has God created us for?"

Enter Man-servant.

MARY IVÁNOVNA [Not listening to her husband, turns to Servant] Bring some boiled cream.

NICHOLAS IVÁNOVICH. And in the Gospels I found the answer, that we certainly should not live for our own sake. That revealed itself to me very clearly once, when I was pondering over the parable of the labourers in the vineyard. You know?

MARY IVÁNOVNA. Yes, the labourers.

NICHOLAS IVÁNOVICH. That parable seemed to show me more clearly than anything else where my mistake had been. Like those labourers I had thought that the vineyard was my own, and that my life was my own, and everything seemed dreadful; but as soon as I had understood that my life is not my own, but that I am sent into the world to do the will of God ...

MARY IVÁNOVNA. But what of it? We all know that!

NICHOLAS IVÁNOVICH. Well, if we know it we cannot go on living as we are doing, for our whole life--far from being a fulfilment of His will--is, on the contrary, a continual transgression of it.

MARY IVÁNOVNA. But how is it a transgression--when we live without doing harm to anyone?

NICHOLAS IVÁNOVICH. But are we doing no harm? Such an outlook on life is just like that of those labourers. Why we ...

MARY IVÁNOVNA. Yes, I know the parable--and that he paid them all equally.

NICHOLAS IVÁNOVICH [after a pause] No, it's not that. But do, Mary, consider one thing--that we have only one life, and can live it well, or can waste it.

MARY IVÁNOVNA. I can't think and argue! I don't sleep at night; I am nursing. I have to manage the whole house, and instead of helping me, you say things to me that I don't understand.

NICHOLAS IVÁNOVICH. Mary!

MARY IVÁNOVNA. And now these visitors.

NICHOLAS IVÁNOVICH. No, let us come to an understanding. [Kisses her] Shan't we?

MARY IVÁNOVNA. Yes, only be like you used to be.

NICHOLAS IVÁNOVICH. I can't, but now listen.

The sound of bells and an approaching vehicle are heard.

MARY IVÁNOVNA. I can't now--they have arrived! I must go to meet them. [Exit behind corner of house. Styópa and Lyúba follow her].

VÁNYA. We shan't abandon it; we must finish the game later. Well, Lyúba, what now?

LYÚBA [seriously] No nonsense, please.

Alexándra Ivánovna, with her husband and Lisa, come out on to the verandah. Nicholas Ivánovich paces up and down wrapt in thought.

ALEXÁNDRA IVÁNOVNA. Well, have you convinced her?

NICHOLAS IVÁNOVICH. Alína, what is going on between us is very important. Jokes are out of place. It is not I who am convincing her, but life, truth, God: they are convincing her--therefore she cannot help being convinced, if not to-day then to-morrow, if not to-morrow ... It is awful that no one ever has time. Who is it that has just come?

PETER SEMYÓNOVICH. It's the Cheremshánovs. Catiche Cheremshánov, whom I have not met for eighteen years. The last time I saw her we sang together: "La ci darem la mano." [Sings].

ALEXÁNDRA IVÁNOVNA. Please don't interrupt us, and don't imagine that I shall quarrel with Nicholas. I am telling the truth. [To Nicholas Ivánovich] I am not joking at all, but it seemed to me strange that you wanted to convince Mary just when she had made up her mind to have it out with you!

NICHOLAS IVÁNOVICH. Very well, very well. They are coming. Please tell Mary I shall be in my room. [Exit].

Curtain.

ACT II
SCENE 1

In the same country-house, a week later. The scene represents a large dining-hall. The table is laid for tea and coffee, with a samovár. A grand piano and a music-stand are by the wall. Mary Ivánovna, the Princess and Peter Semyónovich are seated at the table.

PETER SEMYÓNOVICH. Ah, Princess, it does not seem so long ago since you were singing Rosina's part, and I ... though nowadays I am not fit even for a Don Basilio.

PRINCESS. Our children might do the singing now, but times have changed.

PETER SEMYÓNOVICH. Yes, these are matter-of-fact times ... But your daughter plays really seriously and well. Where are the young folk? Not asleep still, surely?

MARY IVÁNOVNA. Yes, they went out riding by moonlight last night, and returned very late. I was nursing baby and heard them.

PETER SEMYÓNOVICH. And when will my better-half be back? Have you sent the coachman for her?

MARY IVÁNOVNA. Yes, they went for her quite early; I expect she will be here soon.

PRINCESS. Did Alexándra Ivánovna really go on purpose to fetch Father Gerásim?

MARY IVÁNOVNA. Yes, the idea occurred to her yesterday, and she was off at once.

PRINCESS. *Quelle énergie! Je l'admire.*[26]

[26] What energy, I do admire her.

PETER SEMYÓNOVICH. *Oh, pour ceci, ce n'est pas ça qui nous manque.*[27] [Takes out a cigar] But I will go and have a smoke and take a stroll through the park with the dogs till the young people are up. [Exit].

[27] Oh, as far as that goes, we are not lacking.

PRINCESS. I don't know, dear Mary Ivánovna, whether I am right, but it seems to me that you take it all too much to heart. I understand him. He is in a very exalted state of mind. Well, even supposing he does give to the poor? Don't we anyway think too much about ourselves?

MARY IVÁNOVNA. Yes, if that were all, but you don't know him; nor all he is after. It is not simply helping the poor, but a complete revolution, the destruction of everything.

PRINCESS. I do not wish to intrude into your family life, but if you will allow me ...

MARY IVÁNOVNA. Not at all--I look upon you as one of the family--especially now.

PRINCESS. I should advise you to put your demands to him openly and frankly, and to come to an agreement as to the limits ...

MARY IVÁNOVNA [excitedly] There are no limits! He wants to give away everything. He wishes me now, at my age, to become a cook and a washerwoman.

PRINCESS. No, is it possible! That is extraordinary.

MARY IVÁNOVNA [takes a letter out of her pocket] We are by ourselves and I am glad to tell you all about it. He wrote me this letter yesterday. I will read it to you.

PRINCESS. What? He lives in the same house with you, and writes you letters? How strange!

MARY IVÁNOVNA. No, I understand him there. He gets so excited when he speaks. I have for some time past felt anxious about his health.

PRINCESS. What did he write?

MARY IVÁNOVNA. This [reading] "You reproach me for upsetting our former way of life, and for not giving you anything new in exchange, and not saying how I should like to arrange our family affairs. When we begin to discuss it we both get excited, and that's why I am writing to you. I have often told you already why I cannot continue to live as we have been doing; and I cannot, in a letter, show you why that is so, nor why we must live in accord to Christ's teaching. You can do one of two things: either believe in the truth and voluntarily go with me, or believe in me and trusting yourself entirely to me--follow me." [Stops reading] I can do neither the one nor the other. I do not consider it necessary to live as he wishes us to. I have to consider the children, and I cannot rely on him. [Reads] "My plan is this: We shall give our land to the peasants, retaining only 135 acres besides the orchards and kitchen-garden and the meadow by the river. We will try to work ourselves, but will not force one another, nor the children. What we keep should still bring us in about £50 a year."

PRINCESS. Live on £50 a year--with seven children! Is it possible!

MARY IVÁNOVNA. Well, here follows his whole plan: to give up the house and have it turned into a school, and ourselves to live in the gardener's two-roomed cottage.

PRINCESS. Yes, now I begin to see that there is something abnormal about it. What did you answer?

MARY IVÁNOVNA. I told him I couldn't; that were I alone I would follow him anywhere, but I have the children.... Only think! I am still nursing little Nicholas. I tell him we can't break up everything like that. After all, was that what I agreed to when I married? And now I am no longer young or strong. Think what it has meant to bear and nurse nine children.

PRINCESS. I never dreamed that things had gone so far.

MARY IVÁNOVNA. That is how things are and I don't know what will happen. Yesterday he excused the Dmítrovka peasants their rent; and he wants to give the land to them altogether.

PRINCESS. I do not think you should allow it. It is your duty to protect your children. If he cannot deal with the estate, let him hand it over to you.

MARY IVÁNOVNA. But I don't want that.

PRINCESS. You ought to take it for the children's sake. Let him transfer the property to you.

MARY IVÁNOVNA. My sister Alexándra told him so; but he says he has no right to do it; and that the land belongs to those who work it, and that it is his duty to give it to the peasants.

PRINCESS. Yes, now I see that the matter is far more serious than I thought.

MARY IVÁNOVNA. And the Priest! The Priest takes his side, too.

PRINCESS. Yes, I noticed that yesterday.

MARY IVÁNOVNA. That's why my sister has gone to Moscow. She wanted to talk things over with a lawyer, but chiefly she went to fetch Father Gerásim that he may bring his influence to bear.

PRINCESS. Yes, I do not think that Christianity calls upon us to ruin our families.

MARY IVÁNOVNA. But he will not believe even Father Gerásim. He is so firm; and when he talks, you know, I can't answer him. That's what is so terrible, that it seems to me he is right.

PRINCESS. That is because you love him.

MARY IVÁNOVNA. I don't know, but it's terrible, and everything remains unsettled--and that is Christianity!

Enter Nurse.

NURSE. Will you please come. Little Nicholas has woke up and is crying for you.

MARY IVÁNOVNA. Directly! When I am excited he gets stomach ache. Coming, coming!

Nicholas Ivánovich enters by another door, with a paper in his hand.

NICHOLAS IVÁNOVICH. No, this is impossible!

MARY IVÁNOVNA. What has happened?

NICHOLAS IVÁNOVICH. Why, Peter is to be imprisoned on account of some wretched pine-trees of ours.

MARY IVÁNOVNA. How's that?

NICHOLAS IVÁNOVICH. Quite simply! He cut it down, and they informed the Justice of Peace, and he has sentenced him to three months' imprisonment. His wife has come about it.

MARY IVÁNOVNA. Well, and can't anything be done?

NICHOLAS IVÁNOVICH. Not now. The only way is not to possess any forest. And I will not possess any. What is one to do? I shall, however, go and see whether what we have done can be remedied. [Goes out on to the verandah and meets Borís and Lyúba].

LYÚBA. Good morning, papa [kisses him], where are you going?

NICHOLAS IVÁNOVICH. I have just returned from the village and am going back again. They are just dragging a hungry man to prison because he ...

LYÚBA. I suppose it's Peter?

NICHOLAS IVÁNOVICH. Yes, Peter. [Exit, followed by Mary Ivánovna].

LYÚBA [sits down in front of samovár] Will you have tea or coffee?

BORÍS. I don't mind.

LYÚBA. It's always the same, and I see no end to it!

BORÍS. I don't understand him. I know the people are poor and ignorant and must be helped, but not by encouraging thieves.

LYÚBA. But how?

BORÍS. By our whole activity. By using all our knowledge in their service, but not by sacrificing one's own life.

LYÚBA. And papa says, that that is just what is wanted.

BORÍS. I don't understand. One can serve the people without ruining one's own life. That is the way I want to arrange my life. If only you ...

LYÚBA. I want what you want, and am not afraid of anything.

BORÍS. How about those earrings--that dress ...

LYÚBA. The earrings can be sold and the dresses must be different, but one need not make oneself quite a guy.

BORÍS. I should like to have another talk with him. Do you think I should disturb him if I followed him to the village?

LYÚBA. Not at all. I see he has grown fond of you, and he addressed himself chiefly to you last night.

BORÍS [finishes his coffee] Well, I'll go then.

LYÚBA. Yes, do, and I'll go and wake Lisa and Tónya.

Curtain.

SCENE 2

Village street. Iván Zyábrev, covered with a sheepskin coat, is lying near a hut.

IVÁN ZYÁBREV. Maláshka!

A tiny girl comes out of the hut with a baby in her arms. The baby is crying.

IVÁN ZYÁBREV. Get me a drink of water.

Maláshka goes back into the hut, from where the baby can be heard screaming. She brings a bowl of water.

IVÁN ZYÁBREV. Why do you always beat the youngster and make him howl? I'll tell mother.

MALÁSHKA. Tell her then. It's hunger makes him howl!

IVÁN ZYÁBREV [drinks] You should go and ask the Démkins for some milk.

MALÁSHKA. I went, but there wasn't any. And there was no one at home.

IVÁN ZYÁBREV. Oh! if only I could die! Have they rung for dinner?

MALÁSHKA. They have. Here's the master coming.

Enter Nicholas Ivánovich.

NICHOLAS IVÁNOVICH. Why have you come out here?

IVÁN ZYÁBREV. Too many flies in there, and it's too hot.

NICHOLAS IVÁNOVICH. Then you're warm now?

IVÁN ZYÁBREV. Yes, now I'm burning all over.

NICHOLAS IVÁNOVICH. And where is Peter? Is he at home?

IVÁN ZYÁBREV. At home, at this time? Why, he's gone to the field to cart the corn.

NICHOLAS IVÁNOVICH. And I hear that they want to put him in prison.

IVÁN ZYÁBREV. That's so, the Policeman has gone to the field for him.

Enter a pregnant Woman, carrying a sheaf of oats and a rake. She immediately hits Maláshka on the back of the head.

WOMAN. What d'you mean by leaving the baby? Don't you hear him howling! Running about the streets is all *you* know.

MALÁSHKA [howling] I've only just come out. Daddy wanted a drink.

WOMAN. I'll give it you. [She sees the land-owner, N. I. Saryntsov] Good-day, sir. Children are a trouble! I'm quite done up, everything on my shoulders, and now they're taking our only worker to prison, and this lout is sprawling about here.

NICHOLAS IVÁNOVICH. What are you saying? He's quite ill!

WOMAN. He's ill, and what about me? Am I not ill? When it's work, he's ill; but to merry-make or pull my hair out, he's not too ill. Let him die like a hound! What do I care?

NICHOLAS IVÁNOVICH. How can you say such wicked things?

WOMAN. I know it's a sin; but I can't subdue my heart. I'm expecting another child, and I have to work for two. Other people have their harvest in already, and we have not mowed a quarter of our oats yet. I ought to finish binding the sheaves, but can't. I had to come and see what the children were about.

NICHOLAS IVÁNOVICH. The oats shall be cut--I'll hire someone, and to bind the sheaves too.

WOMAN. Oh, binding's nothing. I can do that myself, if it's only mown down quick. What d'you think, Nicholas Ivánovich, will he die? He is very ill!

NICHOLAS IVÁNOVICH. I don't know. But he really is very ill. I think we must send him to the hospital.

WOMAN. Oh God! [Begins to cry] Don't take him away, let him die here.[28] [To her husband, who utters something] What's the matter?

[28] The woman, for all her roughness, is sorry to part from her husband.

IVÁN ZYÁBREV. I want to go to the hospital. Here I'm treated worse than a dog.

WOMAN. Well, I don't know. I've lost my head. Maláshka, get dinner ready.

NICHOLAS IVÁNOVICH. What have you for dinner?

WOMAN. What? Why, potatoes and bread, and not enough of that. [Enters hut. A pig squeals, and children are crying inside].

IVÁN ZYÁBREV [groans] Oh Lord, if I could but die!

Enter Borís.

BORÍS. Can I be of any use?

NICHOLAS IVÁNOVICH. Here no one can be of use to another. The evil is too deeply rooted. Here we can only be of use to ourselves, by seeing on what we build our happiness. Here is a family: five children, the wife pregnant, the husband ill, nothing but potatoes to eat, and at this moment the question is being decided whether they are to have enough to eat next year or not. Help is not possible. How can one help? Suppose I hire a labourer; who will he be? Just such another man: one who has given up his farming, from drink or from want.

BORÍS. Excuse me, but if so, what are you doing here?

NICHOLAS IVÁNOVICH. I am learning my own position. Finding out who weeds our gardens, builds our houses, makes our garments, and feeds and clothes us. [Peasants with scythes and women with rakes pass by and bow. Nicholas Ivánovich, stopping one of the Peasants] Ermíl, won't you take on the job of carting for these people?

ERMÍL [shakes his head] I would with all my heart, but I can't possibly do it. I haven't carted my own yet. We are off now to do some carting. But is Iván dying?

ANOTHER PEASANT. Here's Sebastian, he may take on the job. I say, Daddy Sebastian! They want a man to get the oats in.

SEBASTIAN. Take the job on yourself. At this time of year one day's work brings a year's food. [The Peasants pass on].

NICHOLAS IVÁNOVICH. They are all half-starved; they have only bread and water, they are ill, and many of them are old. That old man, for instance, is ruptured and is suffering, and yet he works from four in the morning to ten at night, though he is only half alive. And we? Is it possible, realising all this, to live quietly and consider oneself a Christian? Or let alone a Christian--simply not a beast?

BORÍS. But what can one do?

NICHOLAS IVÁNOVICH. Not take part in this evil. Not own the land, nor devour the fruits of their labour. How this can be arranged, I don't yet know. The fact of the matter is--at any rate it was so with me--I lived and did not realise how I was living. I did not realise that I am a son of God and that we are all sons of God--and all brothers. But as soon as I realised it--realised that we have all an equal right to live--my whole life was turned upside down. But I cannot explain it to you now. I will only tell you this: I was blind, just as my people at home are, but now my eyes are opened and I cannot help seeing; and seeing it all, I can't continue to live in such a way. However, that will keep till later. Now we must see what can be done.

Enter Policeman, Peter, his wife, and boy.

PETER [falls at Nicholas Ivánovich's feet] Forgive me, for the Lord's sake, or I'm ruined. How can the woman get in the harvest? If at least I might be bailed out.

NICHOLAS IVÁNOVICH. I will go and write a petition for you. [To Policeman] Can't you let him remain here for the present?

POLICEMAN. Our orders are to take him to the police-station now.

NICHOLAS IVÁNOVICH [to Peter] Well then go, and I'll do what I can. This is evidently my doing. How can one go on living like this? [Exit].

Curtain.

SCENE 3

In the same country-house. It is raining outside. A drawing-room with a grand piano. Tónya has just finished playing a sonata of Schumann's and is sitting at the piano. Styópa is standing by the piano. Borís is sitting. Lyúba, Lisa, Mitrofán Ermílych and the young Priest are all stirred by the music.

LYÚBA. That andante! Isn't it lovely!

STYÓPA. No, the scherzo. Though really the whole of it is beautiful.

LISA. Very fine.

STYÓPA. But I had no idea you were such an artist. It is real masterly play. Evidently the difficulties no longer exist for you, and you think only of the feeling, and express it with wonderful delicacy.

LYÚBA. Yes, and with dignity.

TÓNYA. While *I* felt that it was not at all what I meant it to be. A great deal remained unexpressed.

LISA. What could be better? It was wonderful.

LYÚBA. Schumann is good, but all the same Chopin takes a stronger hold of one's heart.

STYÓPA. He is more lyrical.

TÓNYA. There is no comparison.

LYÚBA. Do you remember his prelude?

TÓNYA. Oh, the one called the George Sand prelude? [Plays the commencement].

LYÚBA. No, not that one. That is very fine, but so hackneyed. Do play this one. [Tónya plays what she can of it, and then breaks off].

TÓNYA. Oh, that is a lovely thing. There is something elemental about it--older than creation.

STYÓPA [laughs] Yes, yes. Do play it. But no, you are too tired. As it is, we have had a delightful morning, thanks to you.

TÓNYA [rises and looks out of window] There are some more peasants waiting outside.

LYÚBA. That is why music is so precious. I understand Saul. Though I'm not tormented by devils, I still understand him. No other art can make one so forget everything else as music does. [Approaches the window. To Peasants] Whom do you want?

PEASANTS. We have been sent to speak to Nicholas Ivánovich.

LYÚBA. He is not in. You must wait.

TÓNYA. And yet you are marrying Borís who understands nothing about music.

LYÚBA. Oh, surely not.

BORÍS [absently] Music? Oh no. I like music, or rather I don't dislike it. Only I prefer something simpler--I like songs.

TÓNYA. But is not this sonata lovely?

BORÍS. The chief thing is, that it is not important; and it rather hurts me, when I think of the lives men live, that so much importance is attached to music.

They all eat sweetmeats, which are standing on the table.

LISA. How nice it is to have a fiancé here and sweetmeats provided!

BORÍS. Oh that is not my doing. It's mamma's.

TÓNYA. And quite right too.

LYÚBA. Music is precious because it seizes us, takes possession of us, and carries us away from reality. Everything seemed gloomy till you suddenly began to play, and really it has made everything brighter.

LISA. And Chopin's valses. They are hackneyed, but all the same ...

TÓNYA. This ... [plays].

Enter Nicholas Ivánovich. He greets Borís, Tónya, Styópa, Lisa, Mitrofán Ermílych and the Priest.

NICHOLAS IVÁNOVICH. Where's mamma?

LYÚBA. I think she's in the nursery.

Styópa calls the Man-servant.

LYÚBA. Papa, how wonderfully Tónya plays! And where have you been?

NICHOLAS IVÁNOVICH. In the village.

Enter servant, Afanásy.

STYÓPA. Bring another samovár.

NICHOLAS IVÁNOVICH [greets the Man-servant, and shakes hands with him[29]] Good-day. [Servant becomes confused. Exit Servant. Nicholas Ivánovich also goes off].

[29] People shake hands much more often in Russia than in England, but it is quite unusual to shake hands with a servant, and Nicholas Ivánovich does it in consequence of his belief that all men are brothers.

STYÓPA. Poor Afanásy! He was terribly confused. I can't understand papa. It is as if we were guilty of something.

Enter Nicholas Ivánovich.

NICHOLAS IVÁNOVICH. I was going back to my room without having told you what I feel. [To Tónya] If what I say should offend you--who are our guest--forgive me, but I cannot help saying it. You, Lisa, say that Tónya plays well. All you here, seven or eight healthy young men and women, have slept till ten o'clock, have eaten and drunk and are still eating; and you play and discuss music: while there, where I have just been, they were all up at three in the morning, and those who pastured the horses at night have not slept at all; and old and young, the sick and the weak, children and nursing-mothers and pregnant women are working to the utmost limits of their strength, so that we here may consume the fruits of their labour. Nor is that all. At this very moment, one of them, the only breadwinner of a family, is being dragged to prison because he has cut down one of a hundred thousand pine-trees that grow in the forest that is called *mine*. And we here, washed and clothed, having left the slops in our bedrooms to be cleaned up by slaves, eat and drink and discuss Schumann and Chopin and which of them moves us most or best cures our ennui? That is what I was thinking when I passed you, so I have spoken. Consider, is it possible to go on living in this way? [Stands greatly agitated].

LISA. True, quite true!

LYÚBA. If one lets oneself think about it, one can't live.

STYÓPA. Why? I don't see why the fact that people are poor should prevent one talking about Schumann. The one does not exclude the other. If one ...

NICHOLAS IVÁNOVICH [angrily] If one has no heart, if one is made of wood ...

STYÓPA. Well, I'll hold my tongue.

TÓNYA. It is a terrible problem; it is the problem of our day; and we should not be afraid of it, but look it straight in the face, in order to solve it.

NICHOLAS IVÁNOVICH. We cannot wait for the problem to be solved by public measures. Every one of us must die--if not to-day, then to-morrow. How can I live without suffering from this internal discord?

BORÍS. Of course there is only one way; that is, not to take part in it at all.

NICHOLAS IVÁNOVICH. Well, forgive me if I have hurt you. I could not help saying what I felt. [Exit].

STYÓPA. Not take part in it? But our whole life is bound up with it.

BORÍS. That is why he says that the first step is to possess no property; to change our whole way of life and live so as not to be served by others but to serve others.

TÓNYA. Well, I see *you* have quite gone over to Nicholas Ivánovich's side.

BORÍS. Yes, I now understand it for the first time--after what I saw in the village.... You need only take off the spectacles through which we are accustomed to look at the life of the people, to realise at once the connection between their sufferings and our pleasures-- that is enough!

MITROFÁN ERMÍLYCH. Yes, but the remedy does not consist in ruining one's own life.

STYÓPA. It is surprising how Mitrofán Ermílych and I, though we usually stand poles asunder, come to the same conclusion: those are my very words, "not ruin one's own life."

BORÍS. Naturally! You both of you wish to lead a pleasant life, and therefore want life arranged so as to ensure that pleasant life for you. [To Styópa] You wish to maintain the present system, while Mitrofán Ermílych wants to establish a new one.

Lyúba and Tónya whisper together. Tónya goes to the piano and plays a nocturne by Chopin. General silence.

STYÓPA. That's splendid; that solves everything.

BORÍS. It obscures and postpones everything!

While Tónya is playing, Mary Ivánovna and the Princess enter quietly and sit down to listen.

Before the end of the nocturne carriage bells are heard outside.

LYÚBA. It is Aunt. [Goes to meet her].

The music continues. Enter Alexándra Ivánovna, Father Gerásim (a priest with a cross round his neck) and a Notary. All rise.

FATHER GERÁSIM. Please go on, it is very pleasant.

The Princess approaches to receive his blessing, and the young Priest does the same.

ALEXÁNDRA IVÁNOVNA. I have done exactly what I said I would do. I found Father Gerásim, and you see I have persuaded him to come--he was on his way to Koursk--so I have done my part; and here is the Notary. He has got the deed ready; it only needs signing.

MARY IVÁNOVNA. Won't you have some lunch?

Notary puts down his papers on the table, and exit.

MARY IVÁNOVNA. I am very grateful to Father Gerásim.

FATHER GERÁSIM. What else could I do--though it was out of my way--yet as a Christian I considered it my duty to visit him.

Alexándra Ivánovna whispers to the young people. They consult together and go out on to the verandah, all except Borís. The young Priest also wants to go.

FATHER GERÁSIM.[30] No. You as a pastor and spiritual father must remain here! You may benefit by it yourself, and may be of use to others. Stay here, if Mary Ivánovna has no objection.

[30] Father Gerásim is modelled on the lines of the celebrated Father John of Cronstadt.

MARY IVÁNOVNA. No, I am as fond of Father Vasíly as if he were one of the family. I have even consulted him; but being so young he has not much authority.

FATHER GERÁSIM. Naturally, naturally.

ALEXÁNDRA IVÁNOVNA [approaching] Well, you see now, Father Gerásim, that you are the only person who can help and can bring him to reason. He is a clever, well-read man, but learning, you know, can only do harm. He is suffering from some sort of delusion. He maintains that the Christian law forbids a man to own any property; but how is that possible?

FATHER GERÁSIM. Temptation, spiritual pride, self-will! The Fathers of the Church have answered the question satisfactorily. But how did this befall him?

MARY IVÁNOVNA. Well, to tell you everything ... when we married he was quite indifferent to religion, and we lived so, and lived happily, during our best years--the first twenty years. Then he began to reflect. Perhaps he was influenced by his sister, or by what he read. Anyhow, he began thinking and reading the Gospels, and then suddenly he grew extremely religious, began going to church and visiting the monks. Then all at once he gave all this up and changed his way of life completely. He began doing manual labour, would not let the servants wait on him, and above all he is now giving away his property. He yesterday gave away a forest--both the trees and land. It frightens me, for I have seven children. Do talk to him. I'll go and ask him whether he will see you. [Exit].

FATHER GERÁSIM. Nowadays many are falling away. And is the estate his or his wife's?

PRINCESS. His! That's what is so unfortunate.

FATHER GERÁSIM. And what is his official rank?

PRINCESS. His rank is not high. Only that of a cavalry captain, I believe. He was once in the army.

FATHER GERÁSIM. There are many who turn aside in that way. In Odessa there was a lady who was carried away by Spiritualism and began to do much harm. But all the same, God enabled us to lead her back to the Church.

PRINCESS. The chief thing, please understand, is that my son is about to marry his daughter. I have given my consent, but the girl is used to luxury and should therefore be provided for, and not have to depend entirely on my son. Though I admit he is a hard-working and an exceptional young man.

Enter Mary Ivánovna and Nicholas Ivánovich.

NICHOLAS IVÁNOVICH. How d'you do, Princess? How d'you do? [To Father Gerásim] I beg your pardon. I don't know your name.[31]

[31] He knows that the priest is Father Gerásim, but wishes to address him not as a priest, but by his Christian name and patronymic, as one gentleman would usually address another.

FATHER GERÁSIM. Do you not wish to receive my blessing?

NICHOLAS IVÁNOVICH. No, I don't.

FATHER GERÁSIM. My name is Gerásim Sédorovitch. Very pleased to meet you.

Men-servants bring lunch and wine.

FATHER GERÁSIM. Pleasant weather, and good for the harvest.

NICHOLAS IVÁNOVICH. I suppose you came, at Alexándra Ivánovna's invitation, to divert me from my errors and direct me in the path of truth. If that is so, don't let us beat about the bush, but let us get to business at once. I do not deny that I disagree with the teaching of the Church. I used to agree with it, and then left off doing so. But with my whole heart I wish to be in the truth and will at once accept it if you show it to me.

FATHER GERÁSIM. How is it you say you don't believe the teaching of the Church? What is there to believe in, if not the Church?

NICHOLAS IVÁNOVICH. God and His law, given to us in the Gospels.

FATHER GERÁSIM. The Church teaches that very law.

NICHOLAS IVÁNOVICH. If it did so, I should believe in the Church, but unfortunately it teaches the contrary.

FATHER GERÁSIM. The Church cannot teach the contrary, because it was established by the Lord himself. It is written, "I give you power," and, "Upon this rock I will build my Church; and the gates of hell shall not prevail against it."

NICHOLAS IVÁNOVICH. That was not said in this connection at all, and proves nothing. But even if we were to admit that Christ established the Church, how do I know that it was *your* Church?

FATHER GERÁSIM. Because it is said, "Where two or three are gathered together in my name, there am I in the midst of them."

NICHOLAS IVÁNOVICH. That, too, was not said in this connection, and proves nothing.

FATHER GERÁSIM. How *can* one deny the Church? It alone provides salvation.

NICHOLAS IVÁNOVICH. I did not deny the Church until I found it supported everything that is contrary to Christianity.

FATHER GERÁSIM. It can make no mistakes, for it alone has the truth. Those who leave it go astray, but the Church is sacred.

NICHOLAS IVÁNOVICH. I have already told you that I do not accept that. I do not accept it because, as is said in the Gospels, "By their deeds shall ye know them, by their fruit shall ye know them." I have found out that the Church blesses oaths, murders and executions.

FATHER GERÁSIM. The Church acknowledges and sanctifies the Powers ordained by God.

During the conversation, Styópa, Lyúba, Lisa and Tónya at different times enter the room and sit or stand listening.

NICHOLAS IVÁNOVICH. I know that the Gospels say, not only "Do not kill," but "Do not be angry," yet the Church blesses the army. The Gospel says, "Swear not at all," yet the Church administers oaths. The Gospel says ...

FATHER GERÁSIM. Excuse me. When Pilate[32] said, "I adjure thee by the living God," Christ accepted his oath by replying "I am."

[32] Father Gerásim attributes to Pilate what was said by Caiaphas the high priest.

NICHOLAS IVÁNOVICH. Dear me! What are you saying? That is really absurd.

FATHER GERÁSIM. That is why the Church does not permit everyone to interpret the Gospel, lest he should go astray, but like a mother caring for her child gives him an interpretation suitable to his strength. No, let me finish! The Church does not lay on its children burdens too heavy for them to bear, but demands that they should keep the Commandments: love, do no murder, do not steal, do not commit adultery.

NICHOLAS IVÁNOVICH. Yes! Do not kill me, do not steal from me my stolen goods. We have all robbed the people, we have stolen their land and have then made a law forbidding them to steal it back; and the Church sanctions all these things.

FATHER GERÁSIM. Heresy and spiritual pride are speaking through you. You ought to conquer your intellectual pride.

NICHOLAS IVÁNOVICH. It is not pride. I am only asking you what should I do according to Christ's law, when I have become conscious of the sin of robbing the people and enslaving them by means of the land. How am I to act? Continue to own land and to profit by the labour of starving men: putting them to this kind of work [points to Servant who is bringing in the lunch and some wine], or am I to return the land to those from whom my ancestors stole it?

FATHER GERÁSIM. You must act as behoves a son of the Church. You have a family and children, and you must keep and educate them in a way suitable to their position.

NICHOLAS IVÁNOVICH. Why?

FATHER GERÁSIM. Because God has placed you in that position. If you wish to be charitable, be charitable by giving away part of your property and by visiting the poor.

NICHOLAS IVÁNOVICH. But how is it that the rich young man was told that the rich cannot enter the Kingdom of Heaven?

FATHER GERÁSIM. It is said, "If thou wouldest be perfect."

NICHOLAS IVÁNOVICH. But I *do* wish to be perfect. The Gospels say, "Be ye perfect as your Father in Heaven ..."

FATHER GERÁSIM. But we have to understand in what connection a thing is said.

NICHOLAS IVÁNOVICH. I do try to understand, and all that is said in the Sermon on the Mount is plain and comprehensible.

FATHER GERÁSIM. Spiritual pride.

NICHOLAS IVÁNOVICH. Where is the pride, since it is said that what is hidden from the wise is revealed to babes?

FATHER GERÁSIM. Revealed to the meek, but not to the proud.

NICHOLAS IVÁNOVICH. But who is proud? I, who consider myself a man like the rest of mankind, and one who therefore must live like the rest by his own labour and as poorly as his brother men, or those who consider themselves to be specially selected sacred people, knowing the whole truth and incapable of error; and who interpret Christ's words their own way?

FATHER GERÁSIM [offended] Pardon me, Nicholas Ivánovich, I did not come here to argue which of us is right, nor to receive an admonition, but I called, at Alexándra Ivánovna's request, to talk things over with you. But since you know everything better than I do, we had better end our conversation. Only, once again, I must entreat you in God's name to come to your senses. You have gone cruelly astray and are ruining yourself. [Rises].

MARY IVÁNOVNA. Won't you have something to eat?

FATHER GERÁSIM. No, I thank you. [Exit with Alexándra Ivánovna].

MARY IVÁNOVNA [to young Priest] And what now?

PRIEST. Well, in my opinion, Nicholas Ivánovich spoke the truth, and Father Gerásim produced no argument on his side.

PRINCESS. He was not allowed to speak, and he did not like having a kind of debate with everybody listening. It was his modesty that made him withdraw.

BORÍS. It wasn't modesty at all. All he said was so false. It was evident that he had nothing to say.

PRINCESS. Yes, with your usual instability I see that you are beginning to agree with Nicholas Ivánovich about everything. If you believe such things you ought not to marry.

BORÍS. I only say that truth is truth, and I can't help saying it.

PRINCESS. You of all people should not talk like that.

BORÍS. Why not?

PRINCESS. Because you are poor, and have nothing to give away. However, all this is not our business. [Exit, followed by all except Nicholas Ivánovich and Mary Ivánovna].

NICHOLAS IVÁNOVICH [sits pondering, then smiles at his own thoughts] Mary! What is all this for? Why did you invite that wretched, erring man? Why do those noisy women and that priest come into our most intimate life? Can we not settle our own affairs?

MARY IVÁNOVNA. What am I to do, if you want to leave the children penniless? That is what I cannot quietly submit to. You know that I am not grasping, and that I want nothing for myself.

NICHOLAS IVÁNOVICH. I know, I know and believe it. But the misfortune is that you do not trust the truth. I know you see it, but you can't make up your mind to rely on it. You rely neither on the truth nor on me. Yet you trust the crowd--the Princess and the rest of them.

MARY IVÁNOVNA. I believe in you, I always did; but when you want to let the children go begging ...

NICHOLAS IVÁNOVICH. That means that you do not rely on me. Do you think I have not struggled and have not feared! But afterwards I became convinced that this course is not only possible but obligatory, and that it is the one thing necessary and good for the children themselves. You always say that were it not for the children you would follow me, but I say that if we had no children we might live as we are doing; we should then only be injuring ourselves, but now we are injuring them too.

MARY IVÁNOVNA. But what am I to do, if I don't understand?

NICHOLAS IVÁNOVICH. And what am I to do? Don't I know why that wretched man--dressed up in his cassock and wearing that cross--was sent for, and why Alexándra Ivánovna brought the Notary? You want me to hand the estate over to you, but I can't. You know that I have loved you all the twenty years we have lived together. I love you and wish you well, and therefore cannot sign away the estate to you. If I sign it away at all, it can only be to give it back to those from whom it has been taken--the peasants. And I can't let things remain as they are, but must give it to them. I'm glad the Notary has come; and I will do it.

MARY IVÁNOVNA. No, that is dreadful! Why this cruelty? Though you think it a sin, still give it to me. [Weeps].

NICHOLAS IVÁNOVICH. You don't know what you are saying. If I give it to you, I cannot go on living with you; I shall have to go away. I cannot continue to live under these conditions. I shall not be able to look on while the life-blood is squeezed out of the peasants and they are imprisoned, in your name if not in mine. So choose!

MARY IVÁNOVNA. How cruel you are! Is this Christianity? It is harshness! I cannot, after all, live as you want me to. I cannot rob my own children and give everything away to other people; and that is why you want to desert me. Well--do so! I see you have ceased loving me, and I even know why.

NICHOLAS IVÁNOVICH. Very well then--I will sign; but, Mary, you demand the impossible of me. [Goes to writing-table and signs] You wished it, but I shall not be able to go on living like this.

Curtain.

ACT III

SCENE 1

The scene is laid in Moscow. A large room. In it a carpenter's bench; a table with papers on it; a book-cupboard; a looking-glass and pictures on the wall behind, with some planks leaning in front of them. A Carpenter and Nicholas Ivánovich wearing a carpenter's apron are working at the bench, planing.

NICHOLAS IVÁNOVICH [takes a board from the vice] Is that all right?

CARPENTER [setting a plane] Not quite, you must do it more boldly--like this.

NICHOLAS IVÁNOVICH. It is easy to say boldly, but I can't manage it.

CARPENTER. But why should your honour trouble to learn to be a carpenter? There are such a lot of us nowadays that we can hardly get a living as it is.

NICHOLAS IVÁNOVICH [at work again] I'm ashamed to lead an idle life.

CARPENTER. Yours is that kind of position. God has given you property.

NICHOLAS IVÁNOVICH. That's just where it is. I don't believe that God gave it, but that some of us have taken it, and taken it from our brother men.

CARPENTER [taken aback] That's so! But still you've no need to do this.

NICHOLAS IVÁNOVICH. I understand that it must seem strange to you that while living in this house where there is such superfluity, I should wish to earn something.

CARPENTER [laughs] No. Everybody knows that gentlefolk want to master everything. Well, now go over it again with the smoothing plane.

NICHOLAS IVÁNOVICH. You won't believe me and will laugh, but still I must tell you that formerly I was not ashamed to live in this way, but now that I believe in Christ's law, which tells us we are all brothers--I am ashamed to live so.

CARPENTER. If you are ashamed of it, give away your property.

NICHOLAS IVÁNOVICH. I wanted to, but failed, and gave it to my wife.

CARPENTER. But after all it would not be possible for you to do it--you are too used to comforts.

[Voice outside the door] Papa, may I come in?

NICHOLAS IVÁNOVICH. You may, you always may.

Enter Lyúba.

LYÚBA. Good-day, Jacob!

CARPENTER. Good-day, Miss!

LYÚBA. Borís has gone to his regiment. I am afraid of what he may do or say there. What do you think?

NICHOLAS IVÁNOVICH. What can I think? He will do what is natural to him.

LYÚBA. It is awful. He has such a short time to serve[33] and may go and ruin his whole life.

[33] The period of compulsory service for a University graduate would be short in any case.

NICHOLAS IVÁNOVICH. He did well not to come to see me. He understands that I can't say anything to him but what he knows himself. He told me that he handed in his resignation because he sees that not only is there no more immoral, lawless, cruel and brutal occupation than this one, the object of which is to kill, but also that there is nothing more degrading and mean than to have to submit implicitly to any man of higher rank who happens to come along. He knows all that.

LYÚBA. That's just why I am afraid. He knows that, and may want to take some action.

NICHOLAS IVÁNOVICH. His conscience--the God that dwells within him--will decide that. Had he come to me I should have given him only one piece of advice: not to do anything in which he is guided by his reason alone--nothing is worse than that--but only to act when his whole being demands it. Now I, for instance, wished to act according to Christ's injunction: to leave father, wife and children and to follow Him, and I left home, but how did it end? It ended by my coming back and living with you in luxury in town. Because I was trying to do more than I had strength for, I have landed myself in this degrading and senseless position: I wish to live simply and to work with my hands, but in these surroundings, with lackeys and porters, it seems a kind of affectation. I see that, even now, Jacob Nikonórych is laughing at me.

CARPENTER. Why should I laugh? You pay me, and give me my tea. I am grateful to you.

LYÚBA. I wonder if I had not better go to him.

NICHOLAS IVÁNOVICH. My dear, my darling, I know you find it hard and are frightened, though you should not be so. After all, I am a man who understands life. Nothing evil can happen. All that appears evil really makes one's heart more joyful; only understand that a man who has started on that path will have to choose, and it sometimes happens that God's side and the Devil's weigh so equally that the scales oscillate, and it is then that the great choice has to be made. At that point any interference from outside is terribly dangerous and tormenting. It is as though a man were making such terrible efforts to draw a weight over a ridge that the slightest touch would cause him to break his back.

LYÚBA. Why should he suffer so?

NICHOLAS IVÁNOVICH. That is as though a mother were to ask why she should suffer. There can be no childbirth without suffering, and it is the same in spiritual life. One thing I can tell you. Borís is a true Christian, and consequently is free, and if you cannot as yet be like him, or believe in God as he does, then believe in God through him.

MARY IVÁNOVNA [behind door] May I come in?

NICHOLAS IVÁNOVICH. You may always come in. What a reception I'm having here to-day.

MARY IVÁNOVNA. Our priest, Vasíly Nikonórovich, has come. He is going to the Bishop, and has resigned his living!

NICHOLAS IVÁNOVICH. Impossible!

MARY IVÁNOVNA. He is here! Lyúba, go and call him! He wants to see you. [Exit Lyúba]. I had another reason for coming. I want to speak to you about Ványa. He behaves abominably, and does his lesson so badly that he can't possibly pass; and when I speak to him he is rude.

NICHOLAS IVÁNOVICH. Mary, you know I am out of sympathy with the whole manner of life you are all leading, and with the education you are giving to the children. It is a terrible question for me, whether I have a right to see them perishing before my very eyes ...

MARY IVÁNOVNA. Then you should suggest something else, something definite. But what do you offer?

NICHOLAS IVÁNOVICH. I cannot say what. But can only say that first we should get rid of all this depraving luxury.

MARY IVÁNOVNA. So that they should become peasants! I cannot agree to that.

NICHOLAS IVÁNOVICH. Then don't consult me. The things that grieve you are natural and inevitable.

Enter Priest and Lyúba. The Priest and Nicholas Ivánovich kiss[34] one another.

[34] It is not unusual among Russians for men-friends to kiss one another; but it is quite unusual for a man of position to kiss a village priest who calls as a visitor--and it indicates great intimacy or great emotion.

NICHOLAS IVÁNOVICH. Is it possible that you have thrown it all up?

PRIEST. I could stand it no longer.

NICHOLAS IVÁNOVICH. I did not expect it so soon.

PRIEST. But it was really impossible. In our calling we cannot be indifferent. We have to hear confessions, and to administer the Sacrament, and when once one has become convinced that it is all not true ...

NICHOLAS IVÁNOVICH. Well, and what now?

PRIEST. Now I am going to the Bishop to be questioned. I am afraid he will exile me to the Solovétsk Monastery. At one time I thought of asking you to help me to escape abroad, but then I considered that it would seem cowardly. Only, there is my wife!

NICHOLAS IVÁNOVICH. Where is she?

PRIEST. She has gone to her father's. My mother-in-law came and took our boy away. That hurt me very much. I should much like ... [pauses, restraining his tears].

NICHOLAS IVÁNOVICH. Well, may God help you! Are you staying with us?

PRINCESS [running into the room] There now, it has happened. He has refused to serve, and has been put under arrest. I have just been there but was not admitted. Nicholas Ivánovich, you must go.

LYÚBA. Has he refused? How do you know?

PRINCESS. I was there myself! Vasíly Andréevich, who is a Member of the Council, told me all about it. Borís just walked in and told them he would serve no longer, would take no oath, and in fact said everything Nicholas Ivánovich has taught him.

NICHOLAS IVÁNOVICH. Princess! Can such things be taught?

PRINCESS. I don't know. Only this is not Christianity! What is your opinion, Father?

PRIEST. I am no longer "Father."

PRINCESS. Well, all the same. However, you are also one of them! No, I cannot leave things in this state. And what cursed Christianity it is that makes people suffer and perish. I hate this Christianity of yours. It's all right for you, who know you won't be touched; but I have only one son, and you have ruined him!

NICHOLAS IVÁNOVICH. Do be calm, Princess.

PRINCESS. Yes you, you have ruined him! And having ruined him, you must save him. Go and persuade him to abandon all this nonsense. It's all very well for rich people, but not for us.

LYÚBA [crying] Papa, what can be done?

NICHOLAS IVÁNOVICH. I will go. Perhaps I can be of some use. [Takes off his apron].

PRINCESS [helping him on with his coat] They would not let me in, but now we will go together and I shall get my way. [Exeunt].

Curtain.

SCENE 2

A Government office. A Clerk is seated at a table, and a Sentinel is pacing up and down. Enter a General with his Adjutant. The Clerk jumps up, the Sentinel presents arms.

GENERAL. Where is the Colonel?

CLERK. Gone to see that new conscript, Your Excellency.

GENERAL. Ah, very well. Ask him to come here to me.

CLERK. Yes, Your Excellency.

GENERAL. And what are you copying out? Isn't it the conscript's evidence?

CLERK. Yes, sir, it is.

GENERAL. Give it here.

The Clerk hands General the paper and exit. The General hands it to his Adjutant.

GENERAL. Please read it.

ADJUTANT [reading] "These are my answers to the questions put to me, namely: (1) Why I do not take my oath. (2) Why I refuse to fulfil the demands of the Government. (3) What induced me to use words offensive not only to the army but also to the Highest Authorities. In reply to the first question: I cannot take the oath because I accept Christ's teaching, which directly and clearly forbids taking oaths, as in St. Matthew's Gospel, ch. 5 vv. 33-37, and in the Epistle of St. James, ch. 5 v. 12."

GENERAL. Of course he must be arguing! Putting his own interpretations!

ADJUTANT [goes on reading] "The Gospel says: 'Swear not at all, but let your yea be yea, and your nay, nay; and what is more than these is of the evil one!' St. James's Epistle says: 'Before all things, brethren, swear not by the heavens nor by the earth, nor by any other oath; but let your yea be yea, and your nay, nay, that ye fall not into temptation!' But apart from the fact that the Bible gives us such clear injunctions not to swear--or even if it contained no such injunctions--I should still be unable to swear to obey the will of men, because as a Christian I must always obey the will of God, which does not always coincide with the will of men."

GENERAL. He must be arguing! If I had my way, there would be none of this.

ADJUTANT [reading] "I refuse to fulfil the demands of men calling themselves the Government, because ..."

GENERAL. What insolence!

ADJUTANT. "Because those demands are criminal and wicked. They demand of me that I should enter the army, and learn and prepare to commit murder, though this is forbidden both in the Old and the New Testaments, and above all by my conscience. To the third question ..."

Enter Colonel followed by Clerk. The General shakes hands with Colonel.

COLONEL. You are reading the evidence?

GENERAL. Yes. Unpardonably insolent language. Well, go on.

ADJUTANT. "To the third question: What induced me to use offensive words before the Court, my answer is: that I was induced to do so by the wish to serve God, and in order to expose the fraud carried on in His name. This desire, I hope to retain till I die, and therefore ..."

GENERAL. Come; that's enough; one can't listen to all this balderdash. The fact is all this sort of thing must be eradicated, and action taken to prevent the people being perverted. [To Colonel] Have you spoken to him?

COLONEL. I have been doing so all the time. I tried to shame him, and also to convince him that it would only be worse for himself, and that he would gain nothing by it. Besides that, I spoke of his relations. He was very excited, but holds to his opinions.

GENERAL. A pity you talked to him so much. We are in the army not to reason, but to act. Call him here!

Exit Adjutant with Clerk.

GENERAL [sits down] No, Colonel, that's not the way. Fellows of this kind must be dealt with in a different manner. Decisive measures are needed to cut off the diseased limb. One maggoty sheep infects the whole flock. In these cases one must not be too squeamish. His being a Prince, and having a mother and a fiancée, is none of our business. We have a soldier before us and we must obey the Tsar's will.

COLONEL. I only thought that we could move him more easily by persuasion.

GENERAL. Not at all--by firmness; only by firmness! I have dealt with men of that sort before. He must be made to feel that he is a nonentity--a grain of dust beneath a chariot wheel, and that he cannot stop it.

COLONEL. Well, we can try!

GENERAL [getting irritable] No need to try! I don't need to try! I have served the Tsar for forty-four years, I have given and am giving my life to the service, and now this fellow wants to teach me and wants to read me theological lectures! Let him take that to the Priest, but to me--he is either a soldier or a prisoner. That's all!

Enter Borís guarded by two Soldiers and followed by Adjutant and Clerk.

GENERAL [pointing with a finger] Place him there.

BORÍS. I need no placing. I shall stand or sit where I like, for I do not recognise your authority.

GENERAL. Silence! You don't recognise authority? I will make you recognise it.

BORÍS [sits down on a stool] How wrong it is of you to shout so!

GENERAL. Lift him, and make him stand!

Soldiers raise him.

BORÍS. That you can do, and you can kill me; but you cannot make me submit ...

GENERAL. Silence, I tell you. Hear what I have to say to you.

BORÍS. I don't in the least want to hear what you have to say.

GENERAL. He is mad! He must be taken to the hospital to be examined. That is the only thing to do.

COLONEL. The order was to send him to be examined at the Gendarmes' office.

GENERAL. Well, then, send him there. Only put him into uniform.

COLONEL. He resists.

GENERAL. Bind him. [To Borís] Please hear what I have to say to you. I don't care what happens to you, but for your own sake I advise you, bethink yourself. You will rot in a fortress, and not do any good to anyone. Give it up. Well, you flared up a bit and I flared up. [Slaps him on the shoulder] Go, take the oath and give up all that nonsense. [To Adjutant] Is the Priest here? [To Borís] Well? [Borís is silent] Why don't you answer? Really you had better do as I say. You can't break a club with a whip. You can keep your opinions, but serve your time! We will not use force with you. Well?

BORÍS. I have nothing more to say, I have said all I had to.

GENERAL. There, you see, you wrote that there are such and such texts in the Gospels. Well, the Priest knows all about that. Have a talk with the Priest, and then think things over. That will be best. Good-bye, and I hope "au revoir," when I shall be able to congratulate you on having entered the Tsar's service. Send the Priest here. [Exit, followed by Colonel and Adjutant].

BORÍS [To Clerk and Convoy Soldiers] There you see how they deceive you. They know that they are deceiving you. Don't submit to them. Lay down your rifles and go away. Let them put you into the Disciplinary Battalions and flog you; it will not be as bad as it is to serve such impostors.

CLERK. But how could one get on without an army? It's impossible.

BORÍS. That is not for us to consider. We have to consider what God demands of us; and God wants us.

ONE OF THE SOLDIERS. But how is it that they speak of "the Christian army"?

BORÍS. That is not said anywhere in the Bible. It's these impostors who invented it.

Enter a Gendarme Officer with Clerk.

GENDARME OFFICER. Is it here that the conscript, Prince Cheremshánov, is being kept?

CLERK. Yes, sir. Here he is.

GENDARME OFFICER. Come here, please. Are you Prince Borís Siménovich Cheremshánov, who refuses to take the oath?

BORÍS. I am.

GENDARME OFFICER [sits down and points to a seat opposite] Please sit down.

BORÍS. I think our conversation will be quite useless.

GENDARME OFFICER. I don't think so. At any rate not useless to you. You see it's like this. I am informed that you refuse military service and the oath, and are therefore suspected of belonging to the Revolutionary Party, and that is what I have to investigate. If it is true, we shall have to withdraw you from the service and imprison you or banish you according to the share you have taken in the revolution. If it is not true, we shall leave you to the military authorities. You see I express myself quite frankly to you, and I hope you will treat us in the same way.

BORÍS. In the first place I cannot trust men who wear this sort of thing [pointing to the Gendarme Officer's uniform]. Secondly, your very occupation is one I cannot respect, and for which I have the greatest aversion. But I do not refuse to answer your questions. What do you wish to know?

GENDARME OFFICER. In the first place, tell me your name, your calling, and your religion?

BORÍS. You know all that and I will not reply. Only one of the questions is of great importance to me. I am *not* what is called an Orthodox Christian.

GENDARME OFFICER. What then is your religion?

BORÍS. I do not label it.

GENDARME OFFICER. But still?...

BORÍS. Well then, the Christian religion, according to the Sermon on the Mount.

GENDARME OFFICER. Write it down [Clerk writes. To Borís] Still you recognise yourself as belonging to some nationality or rank.

BORÍS. No, I don't. I recognise myself as a man, and a servant of God.

GENDARME OFFICER. Why don't you consider yourself a member of the Russian Empire?

BORÍS. Because I do not recognise any empires.

GENDARME OFFICER. What do you mean by not recognising? Do you wish to overthrow them?

BORÍS. Certainly I wish it, and work for it.

GENDARME OFFICER [To Clerk] Put that down. [To Borís] How do you work for it?

BORÍS. By exposing fraud and lies, and by spreading the truth. When you entered I was telling these soldiers not to believe in the fraud into which they have been drawn.

GENDARME OFFICER. But beside this method of exposing and persuading, do you approve of any others?

BORÍS. No, I not only disapprove, but I consider all violence to be a great sin; and not only violence, but all concealment and craftiness ...

GENDARME OFFICER. Write that down. Very well. Now kindly let me know whom you are acquainted with. Do you know Ivashénko?

BORÍS. No.

GENDARME OFFICER. Klein?

BORÍS. I have heard of him, but never met him.

Enter Priest (an old man wearing a cross and carrying a Bible). The Clerk goes up to him and receives his blessing.

GENDARME OFFICER. Well, I think I may stop. I consider that you are not dangerous, and not within our jurisdiction. I wish you a speedy release. Good-day. [Presses Borís's hand].

BORÍS. One thing I should like to say to you. Forgive me, but I can't help saying it. Why have you chosen this wicked, cruel profession? I should advise you to give it up.

GENDARME OFFICER [smiles] Thank you for your advice, but I have my reasons. My respects to you. [To Priest] Father, I relinquish my place to you [Exit with Clerk].

PRIEST. How can you so grieve the authorities by refusing to fulfil the duty of a Christian, to serve the Tsar and your Fatherland?

BORÍS [smiling] Just because I want to fulfil my duty as a Christian, I do not wish to be a soldier.

PRIEST. Why don't you wish it? It is said that, "To lay down one's life for a friend" is to be a true Christian....

BORÍS. Yes, to "lay down one's life," but not to take another man's. That is just what I want to do, to "lay down my life."

PRIEST. You do not reason rightly, young man. John the Baptist said to the soldiers ...

BORÍS [smiling] That only goes to prove that even in those days the soldiers used to rob, and he told them not to!

PRIEST. Well, but why don't you wish to take your oath?

BORÍS. You know that the Gospels forbid it!

PRIEST. Not at all. You know that when Pilate said: "I adjure thee by the living God, art thou the Christ?" the Lord Jesus Christ answered "I am." That proves that oaths are not forbidden.

BORÍS. Are not you ashamed to talk so? You--an old man.

PRIEST. Take my advice and don't be obstinate. You and I cannot change the world. Just take your oath and you'll be at ease. Leave it to the Church to know what is a sin and what is not.

BORÍS. Leave it to you? Are you not afraid to take so much sin upon yourself?

PRIEST. What sin? Having been brought up firmly in the faith, and having worked as a priest for thirty years, I can have no sins on my shoulders.

BORÍS. Whose then is the sin, when you deceive such numbers of people? What have these poor fellows got in their heads? [Points to Sentinel].

PRIEST. You and I, young man, will never settle that. It is for us to obey those placed above us.

BORÍS. Leave me alone! I am sorry for you and--I confess--it disgusts me to listen to you. Now if you were like that General--but you come here with a cross and the Testament to persuade me in the name of Christ, to deny Christ! Go [excitedly]. Leave me--Go. Let me be taken back to the cell that I may not see anyone. I am tired, dreadfully tired!

PRIEST. Well, if that is so, good-bye.

Enter Adjutant.

ADJUTANT. Well?

PRIEST. Great obstinacy, great insubordination.

ADJUTANT. So he has refused to take the oath and to serve?

PRIEST. On no account will he.

ADJUTANT. Then he must be taken to the hospital.

PRIEST. And reported as ill? That no doubt would be better, or his example may lead others astray.

ADJUTANT. To be put under observation in the ward for the mentally diseased. Those are my orders.

PRIEST. Certainly. My respects to you. [Exit].

ADJUTANT [approaches Borís] Come, please. My orders are to conduct you----

BORÍS. Where to?

ADJUTANT. First of all to the hospital, where it will be quieter for you, and where you will have time to think things over.

BORÍS. I've thought them over long ago. But let us go! [Exeunt].

Curtain.

SCENE 3

Room in Hospital. Head Doctor, Assistant Doctor, an Officer-Patient in a dressing-gown, and two Warders wearing blouses.

PATIENT. I tell you that you are only leading me to perdition. I have already several times felt quite well.

HEAD DOCTOR. You must not get excited. I should be glad to sign an order for you to leave the hospital, but you know yourself that liberty is dangerous for you. If I were sure that you would be looked after ...

PATIENT. You think I should take to drink again? No, I have had my lesson, but every extra day I spend here only does me harm. You are doing [gets excited] the opposite of what you ought to do. You are cruel. It's all very well for *you*!

HEAD DOCTOR. Don't get excited. [Makes a sign to Warders; who come up from behind].

PATIENT. It's easy for you to argue, being at liberty; but how about us who are kept among madmen! [To Warders] What are you after? Be off!

HEAD DOCTOR. I beg of you to be calm.

PATIENT. But I beg and I demand that you set me free. [Yells, and rushes at the Doctor, but the Warders seize him. A struggle; after which he is taken out].

ASSISTANT DOCTOR. There! Now it has begun again. He nearly got at you that time.

HEAD DOCTOR. Alcoholic ... nothing can be done. But there is some improvement.

Enter Adjutant.

ADJUTANT. How d'you do.

HEAD DOCTOR. Good morning!

ADJUTANT. I have brought you an interesting fellow, a certain Prince Cheremshánov, who has been conscripted, but on religious grounds refuses to serve. He was sent to the Gendarmes, but they say he does not come within their jurisdiction, not being a political conspirator. The Priest exhorted him, but also without effect.

HEAD DOCTOR [laughing] And then as usual you bring him to us, as the highest Court of Appeal. Well, let's have him.

Exit Assistant Doctor.

ADJUTANT. He is said to be a highly educated young man, and he is engaged to a rich girl. It's extraordinary! I really consider this is the right place for him!

HEAD DOCTOR. Yes, it's a mania.

Borís is brought in.

HEAD DOCTOR. Glad to see you. Please take a seat and let's have a chat. [To Adjutant] Please leave us. [Exit Adjutant].

BORÍS. I should like to ask you, if possible, if you mean to lock me up somewhere, to be so good as to do it quickly and let me rest.

HEAD DOCTOR. Excuse me, we must keep the rules. Only a few questions. What do you feel? What are you suffering from?

BORÍS. Nothing. I am perfectly well.

HEAD DOCTOR. Yes, but you are not behaving like other people.

BORÍS. I am behaving as my conscience demands.

HEAD DOCTOR. Well, you see you have refused to perform your military service. On what grounds do you do so?

BORÍS. I am a Christian, and therefore cannot commit murder.

HEAD DOCTOR. But one must defend one's country from her foes, and keep those who want to destroy the social order from evil-doing.

BORÍS. No one is attacking our country; and there are more among the governors who destroy social order, than there are among those whom they oppress.

HEAD DOCTOR. Yes? But what do you mean by that?

BORÍS. I mean this: the chief cause of evil--vódka--is sold by the Government; false and fraudulent religion is also fostered by the Government; and this military service which they demand of me-- and which is the chief means of demoralising the people--is also demanded by the Government.

HEAD DOCTOR. Then, in your opinion, Government and the State are unnecessary.

BORÍS. That I don't know; but I know for certain that I must take no part in evil-doing.

HEAD DOCTOR. But what is to become of the world? Is not our reason given in order to enable us to look ahead.

BORÍS. It is also given in order to enable us to see that social order should not be maintained by violence, but by goodness; and that one man's refusal to participate in evil cannot be at all dangerous.

HEAD DOCTOR. Well now, allow me to examine you a bit. Will you have the goodness to lie down? [Begins touching him] You feel no pain here?

BORÍS. No.

HEAD DOCTOR. Nor here?

BORÍS. No.

HEAD DOCTOR. Take a deep breath, please. Now don't breathe. Now allow me [takes out a measure and measures forehead and nose]. Now be so good as to shut your eyes and walk.

BORÍS. Are you not ashamed to do all this?

HEAD DOCTOR. What do you mean?

BORÍS. All this nonsense? You know that I am quite well and that I am sent here because I refuse to take part in their evil deeds, and because they have no answer to give to the truth I told them; and that is why they pretend to think me mad. And you co-operate with them. It is horrid and it is shameful. Don't do it!

HEAD DOCTOR. Then you don't wish to walk?

BORÍS. No, I don't. You may torture me, but you must do it yourself; I won't help you. [Hotly] Let me alone! [The Doctor presses button of bell. Enter two Warders].

HEAD DOCTOR. Don't get excited. I quite understand that your nerves are strained. Will you please go to your ward?

Enter Assistant Doctor.

ASSISTANT DOCTOR. Some visitors have just come to see Cheremshánov.

BORÍS. Who are they?

ASSISTANT DOCTOR. Sarýntsov and his daughter.

BORÍS. I should like to see them.

HEAD DOCTOR. There is no reason why you shouldn't. Ask them in. You may see them here. [Exit, followed by Assistant and Warders].

Enter Nicholas Ivánovich and Lyúba. The Princess looks in at the door and says, "*Go in, I'll come later.*"

LYÚBA [goes straight to Borís, takes his head in her hands and kisses him] Poor Borís.

BORÍS. No, don't pity me. I feel so well, so joyful, so light. How d'you do. [Kisses Nicholas Ivánovich].

NICHOLAS IVÁNOVICH. I have come to say chiefly one thing to you. First of all, in such affairs it is worse to overdo it than not to do enough. And in this matter you should do as is said in the Gospels, and not think beforehand, "I shall say this, or do that": "When they deliver you up, take no thought how or what ye shall speak: for it is not ye that speak, but the Spirit of your Father who speaketh in you." That is to say, do not act because you have reasoned out beforehand that you should do so and so, but act only when your whole being feels that you cannot act otherwise.

BORÍS. I have done so. I did not think I should refuse to serve; but when I saw all this fraud, those Mirrors of Justice, those Documents, the Police and Officers smoking, I could not help saying what I did. I was frightened, but only till I had begun, after that it was all so simple and joyful.

Lyúba sits down and cries.

NICHOLAS IVÁNOVICH. Above all, do nothing for the sake of being praised, or to gain the approval of those whose opinion you value. For myself I can say definitely, that if you take the oath at once, and enter the service, I shall love and esteem you not less but more than before; because not the things that take place in the external world are valuable, but that which goes on within the soul.

BORÍS. Of course, for what happens within the soul must make a change in the outside world.

NICHOLAS IVÁNOVICH. Well, I have said my say. Your mother is here. She is terribly upset. If you can do what she asks, do it--that is what I wished to say to you.

From the corridor outside hysterical weeping is heard. A Lunatic rushes in, followed by Warders who drag him out again.

LYÚBA. How terrible! And you will be kept here? [Weeps].

BORÍS. I am not afraid of it, I'm afraid of nothing now! I feel so happy, the only thing I fear is what you feel about it. Do help me; I am sure you will!

LYÚBA. Can I be glad about it?

NICHOLAS IVÁNOVICH. Not glad, that is impossible. I myself am not glad. I suffer on his account and would gladly take his place, but though I suffer I yet know that it is well.

LYÚBA. It may be well; but when will they set him free?

BORÍS. No one knows. I do not think of the future. The present is so good, and you can make it still better.

Enter the Princess, his mother.

PRINCESS. I can wait no longer! [To Nicholas Ivánovich] Well, have you persuaded him? Does he agree? Bórya, my darling, you understand, don't you, what I suffer? For thirty years I have lived but for you; rearing you, rejoicing in you. And now when everything has been done and is complete--you suddenly renounce everything. Prison and disgrace! Oh no! Bórya!

BORÍS. Mamma! Listen to me.

PRINCESS [to Nicholas Ivánovich] Why do you say nothing? You have ruined him, it is for you to persuade him. It's all very well for you! Lyúba, do speak to him!

LYÚBA. I cannot!

BORÍS. Mamma, do understand that there are things that are as impossible as flying; and I cannot serve in the army.

PRINCESS. You think that you can't! Nonsense. Everybody has served and does serve. You and Nicholas Ivánovich have invented some new sort of Christianity which is not Christianity, but a devilish doctrine to make everybody suffer!

BORÍS. As is said in the Gospels!

PRINCESS. Nothing of the kind, or if it is, then all the same it is stupid. Darling, Bórya, have pity on me. [Throws herself on his neck, weeps] My whole life has been nothing but sorrow. There was but one ray of joy, and you are turning it into torture. Bórya--have pity on me!

BORÍS. Mamma, this is terribly hard on me. But I cannot explain it to you.

PRINCESS. Come now, don't refuse--say you will serve!

NICHOLAS IVÁNOVICH. Say you will think it over--and do think it over.

BORÍS. Very well then. But you too, Mamma, should have pity on me. It is hard on me too. [Cries are again heard from the corridor]. You know I'm in a lunatic asylum, and might really go mad.

Enter Head Doctor.

HEAD DOCTOR. Madam, this may have very bad consequences. Your son is in a highly excited condition. I think we must put an end to this interview. You may call on visiting days--Thursdays and Sundays. Please come to see him before twelve o'clock.

PRINCESS. Very well, very well, I will go. Bórya, good-bye! Think it over. Have pity on me and meet me next Thursday with good news!

NICHOLAS IVÁNOVICH [shaking hands with Borís] Think it over with God's help, and as if you knew you were to die to-morrow. Only so will you decide rightly. Good-bye.

BORÍS [approaching Lyúba] And what do you say to me?

LYÚBA. I cannot lie; and I do not understand why you should torment yourself and everybody. I do not understand--and can say nothing. [Goes out weeping. Exeunt all except Borís].

BORÍS [alone] Oh how hard it is! Oh, how hard, Lord help me! [Prays].

Enter Warders with dressing-gown.

WARDER. Please change.

Borís puts on dressing-gown.

Curtain.

ACT IV

SCENE 1

In Moscow a year later. A drawing-room in the Saryntsov's town house is prepared for a dance. Footmen are arranging plants round the grand piano. Enter Mary Ivánovna in an elegant silk dress, with Alexándra Ivánovna.

MARY IVÁNOVNA. A ball? No, Only a dance! A "Juvenile Party" as they once used to say. My children took part in the Theatricals at the Mákofs, and have been asked to dances everywhere, so I must return the invitations.

ALEXÁNDRA IVÁNOVNA. I am afraid Nicholas does not like it.

MARY IVÁNOVNA. I can't help it. [To Footmen] Put it here! [To Alexándra Ivánovna] God knows how glad I should be not to cause him unpleasantness. But I think he has become much less exacting.

ALEXÁNDRA IVÁNOVNA. No, no! Only he does not show it so much. I saw how upset he was when he went off to his own room after dinner.

MARY IVÁNOVNA. What can I do? After all, people must live. We have seven children, and if they find no amusement at home, heaven knows what they may be up to. Anyhow I am quite happy about Lyúba now.

ALEXÁNDRA IVÁNOVNA. Has he proposed, then?

MARY IVÁNOVNA. As good as proposed. He has spoken to her, and she has said, Yes!

ALEXÁNDRA IVÁNOVNA. That again will be a terrible blow to Nicholas.

MARY IVÁNOVNA. Oh, he knows. He can't help knowing.

ALEXÁNDRA IVÁNOVNA. He does not like him.

MARY IVÁNOVNA [to the Footmen] Put the fruit on the sideboard. Like whom? Alexander Mikáylovich? Of course not; because he is a living negation of all Nicholas's pet theories. A nice pleasant kindly man of the world. But oh! That terrible night-mare--that affair of Borís Cheremshánov's. What has happened to him?

ALEXÁNDRA IVÁNOVNA. Lisa has been to see him. He is still there. She says he has grown terribly thin, and the Doctors fear for his life or his reason.

MARY IVÁNOVNA. Yes, he is one of the terrible sacrifices caused by Nicholas's ideas. Why need he have been ruined? I never wished it.

Enter Pianist.

MARY IVÁNOVNA [to Pianist] Have you come to play?

PIANIST. Yes, I am the pianist.

MARY IVÁNOVNA. Please take a seat and wait a little. Won't you have a cup of tea?

PIANIST [goes to piano] No, thank you!

MARY IVÁNOVNA. I never wished it. I liked Bórya, but still he was not a suitable match for Lyúba--especially after he let himself be carried away by Nicholas Ivánovich's ideas.

ALEXÁNDRA IVÁNOVNA. But still, the strength of his convictions is astonishing. See what he endures! They tell him that as long as he persists in refusing to serve, he will either remain where he is or be sent to the fortress; but his reply is always the same. And yet Lisa says he is full of joy and even merry!

MARY IVÁNOVNA. Fanatic! But here comes Alexander Mikáylovich!

Enter Alexander Mikáylovich Starkóvsky,[35] an elegant man in evening dress.

[35] Alexander in his Christian name, Mikáylovich (= son of Michael) is his patronymic, and Starkóvsky in his surname which is seldom used in ordinary social life.

STARKÓVSKY. I am afraid I have come too soon. [Kisses the hands of both ladies].

MARY IVÁNOVNA. So much the better.

STARKÓVSKY. And Lyúbov Nikoláyevna?[36] She proposed to dance a great deal so as to make up for the time she has lost, and I have undertaken to help her.

[36] Lyúbov Nikoláyevna (= Love daughter of Nicholas) is the courteous way of naming Lyúba. The latter is a pet name.

MARY IVÁNOVNA. She is sorting favours for the cotillion.

STARKÓVSKY. I will go and help her, if I may?

MARY IVÁNOVNA. Certainly.

As Starkóvsky is going out he meets Lyúba in evening, but not low-necked, dress carrying a cushion with stars and ribbons.

LYÚBA. Ah! here you are. Good! Now you can help me. There are three more cushions in the drawing-room. Go and fetch them all.

STARKÓVSKY. I fly to do so!

MARY IVÁNOVNA. Now, Lyúba; friends are coming, and they will be sure to hint and ask questions. May we announce it?

LYÚBA. No, Mamma, no. Why? Let them ask! Papa will not like it.

MARY IVÁNOVNA. But he knows or guesses; and he will have to be told sooner or later. I think it would be better to announce it to-day. Why, *C'est le secret de la comédie*.[37]

[37] It is only a comedy secret.

LYÚBA. No, no, Mamma, please don't. It would spoil our whole evening. No, no, you must not.

MARY IVÁNOVNA. Well, as you please.

LYÚBA. All right then: after the dance, just before supper.

Enter Starkóvsky.

LYÚBA. Well, have you got them?

MARY IVÁNOVNA. I'll go and have a look at the little ones. [Exit with Alexándra Ivánovna].

STARKÓVSKY [carrying three cushions, which he steadies with his chin, and dropping things on the way] Don't trouble, Lyúbov Nikoláyevna, I'll pick them up. Well, you have prepared a lot of favours. If only I can manage to lead the dance properly! Ványa, come along.

VÁNYA [bringing more favours] This is the whole lot. Lyúba, Alexander Mikáylovich and I have a bet on, which of us will win the most favours.

STARKÓVSKY. It will be easy for you, for you know everybody here, and will gain them easily, while I shall have to charm the young ladies first before winning anything. It means that I am giving you a start of forty points.

VÁNYA. But then you are a fiancé, and I am a boy.

STARKÓVSKY. Well no, I am not a fiancé yet, and I am worse than a boy.

LYÚBA. Ványa, please go to my room and fetch the gum and the pin-cushion from the what-not. Only for goodness' sake don't break anything.

VÁNYA. I'll break everything! [Runs off].

STARKÓVSKY [takes Lyúba's hand] Lyúba, may I? I am so happy. [Kisses her hand] The mazurka is mine, but that is not enough. One can't say much in a mazurka, and I must speak. May I wire to my people that I have been accepted and am happy?

LYÚBA. Yes, to-night.

STARKÓVSKY. One word more: how will Nicholas Ivánovich take it? Have you told him? Yes?

LYÚBA. No, I haven't; but I will. He will take it as he now takes everything that concerns the family. He will say, "Do as you think best." But he will be grieved at heart.

STARKÓVSKY. Because I am not Cheremshánov? Because I am a Maréchal de la Noblesse?

LYÚBA. Yes. But I have struggled with myself and deceived myself for his sake; and it is not because I love him less that I am now doing not what he wants, but it is because I can't lie. He himself says so. I do so want to *live*!

STARKÓVSKY. And life is the only truth! Well, and what of Cheremshánov?

LYÚBA [excitedly] Don't speak of him to me! I wish to blame him, to blame him whilst he is suffering; and I know it is because I feel guilty towards him. All I know is that I feel there is a kind of love--and I think a more real love than I ever felt for him.

STARKÓVSKY. Lyúba, is that true?

LYÚBA. You wish me to say that I love you with that real love--but I won't say it. I do love you with a different kind of love; but it is not the real thing either! Neither the one nor the other is the real thing--if only they could be mixed together!

STARKÓVSKY. No, no, I am satisfied with mine. [Kisses her hand] Lyúba!

LYÚBA [pushes him away] No, let us sort these things. They are beginning to arrive.

Enter Princess with Tónya and a little girl.

LYÚBA. Mamma will be here in a moment.

PRINCESS. Are we the first?

STARKÓVSKY. Some one must be! I have suggested making a gutta-percha dummy to be the first arrival!

Enter Styópa, also Ványa carrying the gum and pin-cushion.

STYÓPA. I expected to see you at the Italian opera last night.

TÓNYA. We were at my Aunt's, sewing for the charity-bazaar.

Enter Students, Ladies, Mary Ivánovna and a Countess.

COUNTESS. Shan't we see Nicholas Ivánovich?

MARY IVÁNOVNA. No, he never leaves his study to come to our gathering.

STARKÓVSKY. Quadrille, please! [Claps his hands. The dancers take their places and dance].

ALEXÁNDRA IVÁNOVNA [approaches Mary Ivánovna] He is terribly agitated. He has been to see Borís, and he came back and saw there was a ball, and now he wants to go away! I went up to his door and overheard him talking to Alexander Petróvich.

MARY IVÁNOVNA. Well?

STARKÓVSKY. *Rond des dames. Les cavaliers en avant!*[38]

[38] Starkóvsky, directing the dance, says: "Ladies form a circle. Gentlemen advance!"

ALEXÁNDRA IVÁNOVNA. He has made up his mind that it is impossible for him to live so, and he is going away.

MARY IVÁNOVNA. What a torment the man is! [Exit].

Curtain.

SCENE 2

Nicholas Ivánovich's room. The dance music is heard in the distance. Nicholas Ivánovich has an overcoat on. He puts a letter on the table. Alexander Petróvich, dressed in ragged clothes, is with him.

ALEXANDER PETRÓVICH. Don't worry, we can reach the Caucasus without spending a penny, and there you can settle down.

NICHOLAS IVÁNOVICH. We will go by rail as far as Túla, and from thence on foot. Well, I'm ready. [Puts letter in the middle of the table, and goes to the door, where he meets Mary Ivánovna] Oh! Why have you come here?

MARY IVÁNOVNA. Why indeed? To prevent your doing a cruel thing. What's all this for? Why d'you do it?

NICHOLAS IVÁNOVICH. Why? Because I cannot continue living like this. I cannot endure this terrible, depraved life.

MARY IVÁNOVNA. It is awful. My life--which I give wholly to you and the children--has all of a sudden become "depraved." [Sees Alexander Petróvich] *Renvoyez au moins cet homme. Je ne veux pas qu'il soit témoin de cette conversation.*[39]

[39] At least send that man away. I don't wish him to be a witness of our conversation.

ALEXANDER PETRÓVICH. *Comprenez. Toujours moi partez.*[40]

[40] Alexander Petróvich replies in very bad French: "I understand! I am always to go away!"

NICHOLAS IVÁNOVICH. Wait for me out there, Alexander Petróvich, I'll come in a minute.

Exit Alexander Petróvich.

MARY IVÁNOVNA. And what can you have in common with such a man as that? Why is he nearer to you than your own wife? It is incomprehensible! And where are you going?

NICHOLAS IVÁNOVICH. I have left a letter for you. I did not want to speak; it is too hard; but if you wish it, I will try to say it quietly.

MARY IVÁNOVNA. No, I don't understand. Why do you hate and torture your wife, who has given up everything for you? Tell me, have I been going to balls, or gone in for dress, or flirted? My whole life has been devoted to the family. I nursed them all myself; I brought them up, and this last year the whole weight of their education, and the managing our affairs, has fallen on me....

NICHOLAS IVÁNOVICH [interrupting] But all this weight falls on you, because you do not wish to live as I proposed.

MARY IVÁNOVNA. But that was impossible! Ask anyone! It was impossible to let the children grow up illiterate, as you wished them to do, and for me to do the washing and cooking.

NICHOLAS IVÁNOVICH. I never wanted that!

MARY IVÁNOVNA. Well, anyhow it was something of that kind! No, you are a Christian, you wish to do good, and you say you love men; then why do you torture the woman who has devoted her whole life to you?

NICHOLAS IVÁNOVICH. How do I torture you? I love you, but ...

MARY IVÁNOVNA. But is it not torturing me to leave me and to go away? What will everybody say? One of two things, either that I am a bad woman, or that you are mad.

NICHOLAS IVÁNOVICH. Well, let us say I am mad; but I can't live like this.

MARY IVÁNOVNA. But what is there so terrible in it, even if once in a winter (and only once, because I feared you would not like it) I do give a party--and even then a very simple one, only ask Mánya and Barbara Vasílyevna! Everybody said I could not do less--and that it was absolutely necessary. And now it seems even a crime, for which I shall have to suffer disgrace. And not only disgrace. The worst of all is that you no longer love me! You love everyone else--the whole world, including that drunken Alexander Petróvich--but I still love you and cannot live without you. Why do you do it? Why? [Weeps].

NICHOLAS IVÁNOVICH. But you don't even wish to understand my life; my spiritual life.

MARY IVÁNOVNA. I do wish to understand it, but I can't. I see that your Christianity has made you hate your family and hate me; but I don't understand why!

NICHOLAS IVÁNOVICH. You see the others do understand!

MARY IVÁNOVNA. Who? Alexander Petróvich, who gets money out of you?

NICHOLAS IVÁNOVICH. He and others: Tónya and Vasíly Nikonórovich. But even if nobody understood it, that would make no difference.

MARY IVÁNOVNA. Vasíly Nikonórovich has repented, and has got his living back, and Tónya is at this very moment dancing and flirting with Styópa.

NICHOLAS IVÁNOVICH. I am sorry to hear it, but it does not turn black into white, and it cannot change my life. Mary! You do not need me. Let me go! I have tried to share your life and to bring into it what for me constitutes the whole of life; but it is impossible.

It only results in torturing myself and you. I not only torment myself, but spoil the work I try to accomplish. Everybody, including that very Alexander Petróvich, has the right to tell me that I am a hypocrite; that I talk but do not act! That I preach the Gospel of poverty while I live in luxury, pretending that I have given up everything to my wife!

MARY IVÁNOVNA. So you are ashamed of what people say? Really, can't you rise above that?

NICHOLAS IVÁNOVICH. It's not that I am ashamed (though I am ashamed), but that I am spoiling God's work.

MARY IVÁNOVNA. You yourself often say that it fulfils itself despite man's opposition; but that's not the point. Tell me, what do you want of me?

NICHOLAS IVÁNOVICH. Haven't I told you?

MARY IVÁNOVNA. But, Nicholas, you know that that is impossible. Only think, Lyúba is now getting married; Ványa is entering the university; Missy and Kátya are studying. How can I break all that off?

NICHOLAS IVÁNOVICH. Then what am I to do?

MARY IVÁNOVNA. Do as you say one should do: have patience, love. Is it too hard for you? Only bear with us and do not take yourself from us! Come, what is it that torments you?

Enter Ványa running.

VÁNYA. Mamma, they are calling you!

MARY IVÁNOVNA. Tell them I can't come. Go, go!

VÁNYA. Do come! [He runs off].

NICHOLAS IVÁNOVICH. You don't wish to see eye to eye--nor to understand me.

MARY IVÁNOVNA. It is not that I don't wish to, but that I can't.

NICHOLAS IVÁNOVICH. No, you don't wish to, and we drift further and further apart. Only enter into my feelings; put yourself for a moment in my place, and you will understand. First, the whole life here is thoroughly depraved. You are vexed with the expression, but I can give no other name to a life built wholly on robbery; for the money you live on is taken from the land you have stolen from the peasants. Moreover, I see that this life is demoralising the children: "Whoso shall cause one of these little ones to stumble," and I see how they are perishing and becoming depraved before my very eyes. I cannot bear it when grown-up men dressed up in swallow-tail coats serve us as if they were slaves. Every dinner we have is a torture to me.

MARY IVÁNOVNA. But all this was so before. Is it not done by everyone--both here and abroad?

NICHOLAS IVÁNOVICH. But *I* can't do it. Since I realised that we are all brothers, I cannot see it without suffering.

MARY IVÁNOVNA. That is as you please. One can invent anything.

NICHOLAS IVÁNOVICH [hotly] It's just this want of understanding that is so terrible. Take for instance to-day! I spent this morning at Rzhánov's lodging-house, among the outcasts there; and I saw an infant literally die of hunger; a boy suffering from alcoholism; and a consumptive charwoman rinsing clothes outside in the cold. Then I returned home, and a footman with a white tie opens the door for me. I see my son--a mere lad--ordering that footman to fetch him some water; and I see the army of servants who work for us. Then I go to visit Borís--a man who is sacrificing his life for truth's sake. I see how he, a pure, strong, resolute man, is deliberately being goaded to lunacy and to destruction, that the Government may be rid of him! I know, and they know, that his heart is weak, and so they provoke him, and drag him to a ward for raving lunatics. It is too dreadful, too dreadful. And when I come home, I hear that the one member of our family who understood--not me but the truth--has thrown over both her betrothed to whom she had promised her love, and the truth, and is going to marry a lackey, a liar ...

MARY IVÁNOVNA. How very Christian!

NICHOLAS IVÁNOVICH. Yes, it is wrong of me, and I am to blame, but I only want you to put yourself in my place. I mean to say that she has turned from the truth ...

MARY IVÁNOVNA. You say, "from the truth"; but other people--the majority--say from "an error." You see Vasíly Nikonórovich once thought he was in error, but now has come back to the Church.

NICHOLAS IVÁNOVICH. That's impossible ----

MARY IVÁNOVNA. He has written to Lisa! She will show you the letter. That sort of conversion is very unstable. So also in Tónya's case; I won't even speak of that fellow Alexander Petróvich, who simply considers it profitable!

NICHOLAS IVÁNOVICH [getting angry] Well, no matter. I only ask *you* to understand me. I still consider that truth is truth! All this hurts me very much. And here at home I see a Christmas-tree, a ball, and hundreds of roubles being spent while men are dying of hunger. I cannot live so. Have pity on me, I am worried to death. Let me go! Good-bye.

MARY IVÁNOVNA. If you go, I will go with you. Or if not with you, I will throw myself under the train you leave by; and let them all go to perdition--and Missy and Kátya too. Oh my God, my God. What torture! Why? What for? [Weeps].

NICHOLAS IVÁNOVICH [at the door] Alexander Petróvich, go home! I am not going. [To his wife] Very well, I will stay. [Takes off his overcoat].

MARY IVÁNOVNA [embracing him] We have not much longer to live. Don't let us spoil everything after twenty-eight years of life together. Well, I'll give no more parties; but do not punish me so.

Enter Ványa and Kátya running.

VÁNYA and KATYA. Mamma, be quick--come.

MARY IVÁNOVNA. Coming, coming. So let us forgive one another! [Exit with Kátya and Ványa].

NICHOLAS IVÁNOVICH. A child, a regular child; or a cunning woman? No, a cunning child. Yes, yes. It seems Thou dost not wish me to be Thy servant in this Thy work. Thou wishest me to be humiliated, so that everyone may point his finger at me and say, "He preaches, but he does not perform." Well, let them! Thou knowest best what Thou requirest: submission, humility! Ah, if I could but rise to that height!

Enter Lisa.

LISA. Excuse me. I have brought you a letter from Vasíly Nikonórovich. It is addressed to me, but he asks me to tell you.

NICHOLAS IVÁNOVICH. Can it be really true?

LISA. Yes. Shall I read it?

NICHOLAS IVÁNOVICH. Please do.

LISA [reading] "I write to beg you to communicate this to Nicholas Ivánovich. I greatly regret the error which led me openly to stray from the Holy Orthodox Church, to which I rejoice to have now returned. I hope you and Nicholas Ivánovich will follow the same path. Please forgive me!"

NICHOLAS IVÁNOVICH. They have tortured him into this, poor fellow. But still it is terrible.

LISA. I also came to tell you that the Princess is here. She came upstairs to me in a dreadfully excited state and is determined to see you. She has just been to see Borís. I think you had better not see her. What good can it do for her to see you?

NICHOLAS IVÁNOVICH. No. Call her in. Evidently this is fated to be a day of dreadful torture.

LISA. Then I'll go and call her. [Exit].

NICHOLAS IVÁNOVICH [alone] Yes--could I but remember that life consists only in serving Thee; and that if Thou sendest a trial, it is because Thou holdest me capable of enduring it, and knowest that my strength is equal to it: else it would not be a trial.... Father, help me--help me to do Thy will.

Enter Princess.

PRINCESS. You receive me? You do me that honour? My respects to you. I don't give you my hand, for I hate you and despise you.

NICHOLAS IVÁNOVICH. What has happened?

PRINCESS. Just this, that they are moving him to the Disciplinary Battalion; and it is you who are the cause of it.

NICHOLAS IVÁNOVICH. Princess, if you want anything, tell me what it is; but if you have come here merely to abuse me, you only injure yourself. You cannot offend me, for with my whole heart I sympathise with you and pity you!

PRINCESS. What charity! What exalted Christianity! No, Mr. Saryntsov, you cannot deceive me! We know you now. You have ruined my son, but you don't care; and you go giving balls; and your daughter--my son's betrothed--is to be married and make a good match, that you approve of; while you pretend to lead a simple life, and go carpentering. How repulsive you are to me, with your new-fangled Pharisaism.

NICHOLAS IVÁNOVICH. Don't excite yourself so, Princess. Tell me what you have come for--surely it was not simply to scold me?

PRINCESS. Yes, that too! I must find vent for all this accumulated pain. But what I want is this: He is being removed to the Disciplinary Battalion, and I cannot bear it. It is you who have done it. You! You! You!

NICHOLAS IVÁNOVICH. Not I, but God. And God knows how sorry I am for you. Do not resist this will. He wants to test you. Bear the trial meekly.

PRINCESS. I cannot bear it meekly. My whole life was wrapped up in my son; and you have taken him from me and ruined him. I cannot be calm. I have come to you--it is my last attempt to tell you that you have ruined him and that it is for you to save him. Go and prevail on them to set him free. Go and see the Governor-General, the Emperor, or whom you please. It is your duty to do it. If you don't do it, I know what I shall do. You will have to answer to me for it!

NICHOLAS IVÁNOVICH. Teach me what to do. I am ready to do anything.

PRINCESS. I again repeat it--you must save him! If you do not--beware! Good-bye. [Exit].

Nicholas Ivánovich (alone). Lies down on sofa. Silence. The door opens and the dance music sounds louder. Enter Styópa.

STYÓPA. Papa is not here, come in!

Enter the adults and the children, dancing in couples.

LYÚBA [noticing Nicholas Ivánovich] Ah, you *are* here. Excuse us.

NICHOLAS IVÁNOVICH [rising] Never mind. [Exit dancing couples].

NICHOLAS IVÁNOVICH. Vasíly Nikonórovich has recanted. I have ruined Borís. Lyúba is getting married. Can it be that I have been mistaken? Mistaken in believing in Thee? No! Father help me!

Curtain.

Tolstoy left the following notes for a fifth act which was never written.

ACT V

Disciplinary Battalion. A cell. Prisoners sitting and lying. Borís is reading the Gospel and explaining it. A man who has been flogged is brought in. "Ah, if there were but a Pugachev[41] to revenge us on such as you." The Princess bursts in, but is turned out. Conflict with an officer. Prisoners led to prayers. Borís sent to the Penitentiary Cell: "He shall be flogged!"

[41] Pugachev was the leader of a formidable rebellion in Russia in the eighteenth century.

Scene changes.

The Tsar's Cabinet. Cigarettes; jokes; caresses. The Princess is announced. "Let her wait." Enter petitioners, flattery, then the Princess. Her request is refused. Exit.

Scene changes.

Mary Ivánovna talks about illness with the doctor. "He has changed, has become more gentle, but is dispirited." Enter Nicholas Ivánovich and speaks to Doctor about the uselessness of treatment. But for his wife's sake he agrees to it. Enter Tónya with Styópa. Lyúba with Starkóvsky. Conversation about land. Nicholas Ivánovich tries not to offend them. Exeunt all. Nicholas Ivánovich with Lisa. "I am always in doubt whether I have done right. I have accomplished nothing. Borís has perished, Vasíly Nikonórovich has recanted. I set an example of weakness. Evidently God does not wish me to be his servant. He has many other servants--and can accomplish his will without me, and he who realises this is at peace." Exit Lisa. He prays. The Princess rushes in and shoots him. Everybody comes running into the room. He says he did it himself by accident. He writes a petition to the Emperor. Enter Vasíly Nikonórovich with Doukhobors.[42] Dies rejoicing that the fraud of the Church is exposed, and that he has understood the meaning of his life.

[42] Tolstoy did not fully realise the facts (described in *A Peculiar People*) of the Doukhobors' submission to their leader, or of their belief in him as an incarnation of the Deity. In fact, when he wrote this play, Tolstoy regarded the Doukhobors as a type of what all Christians should be.

This play was begun in the 'eighties, and continued in 1900 and 1902.

END OF "THE LIGHT SHINES IN DARKNESS."

Printed in Great Britain
by Amazon